CCCC Studies in Writing & Rhetoric

# THE MANAGERIAL UNCONSCIOUS IN THE
# HISTORY OF COMPOSITION STUDIES

# THE MANAGERIAL UNCONSCIOUS

## IN THE HISTORY OF COMPOSITION STUDIES

Donna Strickland

Southern Illinois University Press
*Carbondale and Edwardsville*

14  13  12  11     4  3  2  1

Publication partially funded by a subvention grant
from the Conference on College Composition and
Communication of the National Council of Teachers
of English.

Library of Congress Cataloging-in-Publication Data
   Strickland, Donna.
   The managerial unconscious in the history of com-
position studies / Donna Strickland.
      p. cm. — (Studies in writing & rhetoric)
   Includes bibliographical references and index.
   ISBN-13: 978-0-8093-3026-3 (pbk. : alk. paper)
   ISBN-10: 0-8093-3026-1 (pbk. : alk. paper)
   ISBN-13: 978-0-8093-8629-1 (ebook)
   ISBN-10: 0-8093-8629-1 (ebook)
   1. English language—Rhetoric—Study and teaching.
   2. Writing centers—Administration. I. Title.
   PE1404.S838 2011
   808'.0420711—dc22          2010046778

Printed on recycled paper. ♻
The paper used in this publication meets the minimum
requirements of American National Standard for Information Sciences—Permanence of Paper for Printed
Library Materials, ANSI Z39.48-1992. ∞

*To the memory of my father,*
*Travis Houston Strickland,*
*June 27, 1926–April 27, 2008*

# CONTENTS

## ACKNOWLEDGMENTS

IT TOOK ME AN UNUSUALLY LONG TIME to fully realize just how much I needed others to complete this manuscript. The fact that you are now holding this book is directly linked to the help and support of many people. At the risk of overlooking some (and I need to ask them to forgive me, since I'm certain that I will), I want to acknowledge as many as I can.

First, my debt to Lynn Worsham is huge. She read the earliest versions of some of the ideas that have now matured into chapters of this book. Her intellectual guidance and support have meant the world to me.

Alice Gillam, too, read much earlier versions of some of the chapters here. She also invited me (among others) to join her in inquiring into what it might mean to be a feminist administrator and so laid a foundation for much of the work that I have done.

Jami Carlacio, Ilene Crawford, Christie Launius, Laura Micciche, and Christine Tutlewski were all at various times part of this critical conversation about administration. Their insight and ongoing work have continued to inspire my own. Ilene, my sometime coauthor, deserves very special thanks for so often functioning as the other half of my brain.

Former colleagues at Butler University and Southern Illinois University Carbondale, especially Jane Cogie, Kevin Dettmar, Lisa McClure, and Carol Reeves, supported me with their friendship and interest in my work. I also have deep appreciation for the many graduate students who worked with me during my time at SIUC, especially Chris Drew, Matt Garrison, Steve Leek, Jen Talbot, and Abbey Waldron, who together coauthored an article with me and helped me to think in new ways about the diversity of issues facing graduate teaching assistants.

At the University of Missouri, my current institutional home, I've benefited from many generous colleagues and friends. Rebecca Dingo, in particular, shines in both categories. She and Enid Schatz have spent many hours by my side as we wrote together at one coffeehouse or another. Marty Patton's feedback on an early version of chapter 3 spurred me to think in new ways about what I've included there. Elizabeth Chang, Sam Cohen, and Joanna Hearne have read most every word included here, and I'm hugely indebted to them for their astute suggestions and friendly companionship on the book-writing journey.

And when I say that I don't know if I would have finished this book if I had not met Katie Hogan, I'm not exaggerating. Katie's sincere interest in my work, her encouragement to read Robert Boice's *How Writers Journey to Comfort and Fluency*, and her invitation to join an online writing group came to me at a crucial time. It would be impossible to overstate how much her support has meant to me.

To all the members of the online writing group, too—Lisa Brush, Kirsten Christensen, Linh Hua, Anita McChesney, Sally Poor, Maggie Rehm, and Katie—a tremendous thank you for your faithful presence.

In addition to those already mentioned, a number of my professional colleagues have read various parts (or the whole) of this book, and I'm indebted to each of them for the hand they've had in shaping up this manuscript. Kathryn Flannery read a much earlier version and offered extensive feedback. Her support over the years has been invaluable. (Plus, she introduced me to Katie!) Jeanne Gunner, too, has long supported my research and, as editor of *College English*, published a version of the first chapter. Bruce Horner and Lucy Schultz each offered excellent advice as I was completing this manuscript for the Studies in Writing and Rhetoric series. And Joe Harris, the SWR editor, deserves a huge thanks for his ongoing interest in the book and for his editorial acumen. Thanks also go to Kristine Priddy and the entire SIU Press editorial staff for shepherding it into print.

Various-sized portions of some of the book's chapters have appeared previously. A version of chapter 1 appeared as "Taking Dictation: The Emergence of Writing Programs and the Cultural Contradictions of Composition Teaching," *College English* 63.4 (March 2001; copyright 2001 by the National Council of Teachers of English; used with permission). A small section of chapter 4 was published in "Worrying Democracy: Chantal Mouffe and the Return of Politicized Rhetoric," *JAC: A Journal of Composition Theory* 19 (1999). I'm grateful to the original publishers for permission to reprint these works. In addition, two other previously published pieces touch upon and resonate with various chapters: "The Managerial Unconscious of Composition Studies," *Tenured Bosses and Disposable Teachers: Writing Instruction in the Managed University*, ed. Marc Bousquet, Tony Scott, and Leo Parascondola (Carbondale: Southern Illinois UP, 2004), and "Making the Managerial Conscious in Composition Studies," *American Academic* 1 (2004).

A Research Grant from the Council of Writing Program Administrators provided me with the means to visit the National Council of Teachers of English headquarters in Urbana, Illinois. I would like to thank my research assistant, Jacqueline Gruenwald, and NCTE librarian and archivist Cheri Cameron for their help in locating and securing sources for this project. In addition, a summer grant from the University of Missouri–Columbia Research Council and a semester-long grant from the University of Missouri Research Board provided needed release time for writing.

And many more outside of academia have provided untold spiritual support and guidance through some difficult patches. So it would be unforgivable, really, not to mention how indebted I am for so many things to Carol Koenig, Gregory Kramer, Tonda March, Ginny Morgan, Beth Shoyer, and Sienna (yogini extraordinaire).

On the home front, a number of cats lent a great deal of warmth and a general sense of well-being to the composing process, including the much missed Kitty and Clyde and the current throng consisting of Casey, Gabe, Hansel, and Simon. And to my fellow cat wrangler and dearest companion—Chuck Marvin—thank you for being here with me, through it all.

This book is dedicated to the memory of my father, Travis Strickland. As a young man, he dropped out of high school, served in the navy, and eventually went to work in a rock quarry. His strong work ethic finally led to a position in management. Still, he never stopped saying that he worked for a living. Many years ago, he made a good-faith effort to read my undergraduate honors thesis. I think he might have put forth the same effort to read this book. His love of life and genuine human decency have informed my own life in more ways than I'll ever fully know.

# THE MANAGERIAL UNCONSCIOUS IN THE
# HISTORY OF COMPOSITION STUDIES

# Introduction: Composition Studies' Managerial Unconscious

TO PURSUE A CAREER in composition studies requires a dual schooling: an official schooling in composition pedagogy and rhetorical theories, and a usually unofficial schooling in the management of composition teachers and programs. When I entered a PhD program in rhetoric and composition in the 1990s, I imagined myself becoming an expert in the teaching of writing. A first-generation college student who had become excited about composition while teaching other first-generation college students, I envisioned studying the effects of social class on writing acquisition. What I didn't envision was becoming interpellated into a class system that at the time seemed foreign to me: the hierarchy of contingent teaching faculty and tenure-track administrators that is endemic to writing programs.

When I became the coordinator of the first-semester course in my fourth year of the PhD program, I found myself supervising both fellow graduate student teachers and the non-tenure-track instructors who made less per course than I did as a graduate teaching assistant. So while I was taking classes primarily in rhetorical theory and occasionally in writing pedagogy, a good deal of my time as a graduate student was devoted, in one form or another, to managing other teachers' work: providing orientation to the first-semester course, mentoring new graduate student teachers, observing their classes, facilitating grade norming and portfolio assessment. I also received an informal education in the administrative work and economic constraints of English departments: in the power wielded by financial officers (including one who withheld the budget of the composition program from the program's coordinator, while insisting that it would not allow a course release for a writing center director) and in the influence of deans and upper university administration (many of whom had set in place the required writing placement system and rising junior requirement and later withdrew almost all support for the infrastructure they had demanded). When I went on the job market, as a result of my rather extensive administrative experience, I was, like most composition specialists, a desirable commodity, receiving interview invitations from somewhere in the range of twenty to thirty schools.

And yet, what most of these schools wanted was not so much a specialist in my particular area (the history and ideology of composition studies as a field). Rather, they wanted a writing program administrator, someone to manage a first-year writing program, a writing center, or a writing-across-the-curriculum program. Sometimes I even found myself being asked to direct some combination of these. The ad for the job that I eventually accepted had indicated that I would be put in charge of the first-year program in a few years, but even before my first semester in the job began, I was asked to develop a computer-assisted writing program (something I was only minimally qualified to do). I have held two more tenure-track positions since that one, but since receiving my PhD a decade ago, I have never *not* been involved in writing program administration in some way—helping with orientation and workshops, with grade appeals, with the required pedagogy course or practicum, with curricular changes—even though I have only rarely held an official title like "director" or "coordinator."

If my case is not atypical (and I don't believe it is), it's apparent that my initial assumption about composition studies—that it is a field devoted to questions of writing acquisition and pedagogy—was only partially right. To profess composition, as I have argued elsewhere, is to occupy a position unlike most other professors of English. To profess composition, very often, is to study one thing and to do quite another. In the introduction to their 2002 collection, *The Writing Program Administrator as Theorist*, Shirley K. Rose and Irwin Weiser acknowledge this disjunction: "Until recently, graduate preparation for writing program administration was most often limited to developing a solid grounding in research and theories of rhetoric and composition, with little attention to formal study of writing program administration" (5). The very need to attend to this disjunction between the usual, official schooling provided by and produced in rhetoric and composition graduate programs and the unusual, unofficial one (the one that has often never been provided until after a job is taken) points to what I take to be the "unconscious" of the field of composition studies—the managerial unconscious.

The official schooling provided by the canonical texts of composition studies, moreover—texts including histories and overviews of the field by such important scholars as James Berlin, Robert Connors, Sharon Crowley, and Stephen North—obscured for me the managerial imperative operating in the field. Even as I was actively administrating as a graduate student, I imagined a professional future for myself that would primarily consist of research and teaching. The unconscious that I write of, then, is a discursive one, something unspoken in the most prominent texts in the field even as the people writing the texts may be holding administrative positions.

The recent increase in texts directed toward writing program administrators (WPAs) further supports my view that the fundamental importance of administration to the field has not been acknowledged. Indeed, in asserting that prominent texts in composition studies have not engaged with the managerial, I am purposefully bracketing scholarship produced primarily for an audience of WPAs in particular rather than for the field in general. Since the founding of the Council of Writing Program Administrators in the 1970s and the launching of the council's journal, *WPA: Writing Program Administration*, WPAs have had a dedicated venue for exchanging knowledge. Over the last fifteen years, moreover, a number of important edited collections targeting WPAs have appeared, including Joseph Janangelo and Kristine Hansen's *Resituating Writing: Constructing and Administering Writing Programs*, Diana George's *Kitchen Cooks, Plate Twirlers and Troubadours: Writing Program Administrators Tell Their Stories*, Shirley K. Rose and Irwin Weiser's *The Writing Program Administrator as Researcher: Inquiry in Action and Reflection* and the aforementioned

*The Writing Program Administrator as Theorist: Making Knowledge Work*, Sharon James McGee and Carolyn Handa's *Discord And Direction: The Postmodern Writing Program Administrator*, my own and Jeanne Gunner's *The Writing Program Interrupted: Making Space for Critical Discourse*, and, most recently, Krista Ratcliffe and Rebecca Rickly's *Performing Feminism and Administration in Rhetoric and Composition*. Of particular relevance to my own project is Barbara L'Eplattenier and Lisa Mastrangelo's significant *Historical Studies of Writing Program Administration: Individuals, Communities, and the Formation of a Discipline*. This collection offers historical studies of writing program administration before the founding of the WPA organization. However, as a history of writing program administration rather than of composition studies, it may subtly reinforce the discourse that sees administrative work as a subfield of composition studies, even if an important one. My argument, rather, is that the managerial has been an integral part of the development of the field, so that the history of this function is also a history of the development of composition studies.

In what follows here, I will look more closely at this discursive managerial unconscious, especially as it manifests in histories of the field. I will then turn to the idea of the managerial, which has been the source of much controversy over the last decade, and will finally argue that a history taking the managerial imperative as a framework is long overdue.

## COMPOSITION STUDIES' HISTORICAL UNCONSCIOUS

The history of composition studies has been told primarily as the history of composition pedagogy. The managerial has been largely ignored in the stories codified in the classic histories of composition studies, all written by scholars who focused on the teaching of writing at the very moment that most of them were working as directors of writing programs or centers. These histories of composition studies—for example, Albert Kitzhaber's classic dissertation, James Berlin's two volumes on writing instruction in the nineteenth and twentieth centuries, and Robert Connors's study of composition-rhetoric—have focused primarily on developments in writing pedagogy. While writing and the teaching of writing have indeed been the primary areas of scholarly inquiry over the past thirty years, the working conditions that have supported this scholarship have more often than not involved administration.

In other words, rather than represent composition studies as connected to material, hierarchical workplaces, most histories of composition studies have instead offered histories of ideas, including overviews or critiques of composition pedagogy, that more or less presume an audience of professionally secure teachers. With this emphasis on *ideas* about the teaching of writing, the narratives in these histories have followed idealized trajectories. Hayden White, borrowing from Kenneth Burke's detailing of four master tropes, argues that all histories follow some sort of archetypal narrative, whether tragedy, comedy, romance, or satire. Following from White, I would maintain that much of composition studies' history has been plotted as tragedy, telling of the marginalization of teaching and writing in departments that privilege the interpretation of texts (criticism) over the production of texts (rhetoric) and thus the study of literature over the teaching of writing (Berlin, *Rhetoric and Reality*; Connors, "Rhetoric"). According to this narrative, the status of composition within departments of English has been degraded as a result of the privileging of research over teaching, which is itself described as a result of the overthrow of the traditional liberal arts college by the importation of the German graduate university to the United States (Connors, "Rhetoric"; Brereton, introduction). Composition teaching in the new universities, according to this story, is a fallen and diminished version of the rhetorical education that formerly dominated the curriculum. The only way out of this tragedy, it seems, is to somehow reassert composition's centrality. Thus, Berlin's history of composition instruction becomes an apologia for the composition class, a way of showing that, historically, "the rhetorical training [beginning students] bring with them inevitably proves . . . unequal to the task of dealing with their new intellectual experience" (*Rhetoric and Reality* 3). Further, if the problem of composition's second-class status can be located in the English department's tendency to reward research more than teaching, then the solution ought to involve a rearrangement of departmental priorities; in Connors's words, the English department must see to it that "the work of teaching writing is put on a genuinely equal footing with the other work the department does" ("Rhetoric" 79).

Thus, a more romantic story is told alongside the tragic one, rescuing composition from its degraded and marginal status by repositioning the composition class as a unique site of democratic politics and pedagogical commitment. This narrative typically enshrines certain men—most notably, Fred Newton Scott of the University of Michigan—as heroic figures who refused to accept the marginal status of composition and who blazed a path in quest of a democratic pedagogy. Drawing from this romantic narrative, composition scholars in the 1990s increasingly represented composition studies and the composition class as uniquely counterhegemonic discursive sites. From this "political turn," arguments for the possibility of creating a better society through writing instruction have proliferated. In his 1996 chair's address at the annual Conference on College Composition and Communication, for instance, Lester Faigley maintains, "In a culture that is increasingly cynical about the belief that school should offer equal opportunity to education, we have remained steadfast to the goal of literacy for equality" (41). Similarly, in her essay describing the field of rhetoric and composition in the Modern Language Association's *Introduction to Scholarship*, Andrea Lunsford asserts that the field is "radically democratic" (77). Arguments such as these seem to be based upon the premise of composition's radical difference from the rest of the university curriculum and the rest of society. Even Susan Miller, who argues in *Textual Carnivals* that "composition is an element in, and an active symbol of, hegemonic cultural maintenance" (7), ends up calling for an "intellectual redefinition [that] would re-represent the field as irrefutably counterhegemonic" (186). This romantic narrative has nurtured and has been nurtured by a range of "radical" pedagogies. Ira Shor, for example, a popularizer of Freirean critical pedagogy, has argued that teachers, by creating a student-centered class, can "empower" students: "The act of study," Shor explains, "needs to be thought of as an act of democratization" (96).

The commonplace that serves as the foundation for these tragic and romantic stories is the equating of composition studies with teaching. The field is regarded, in Joseph Harris's words, as a teaching subject, a discipline committed to the practice of teaching. This commitment to teaching—a commitment to students rather than to research—is, according to what Susan Miller has called the "bad story" of composition, the reason the field is marginalized.

What I would like to do is to tell a different kind of story, one that breaks out of the romantic version of composition and goes against the tendency to read the efforts of composition specialists as necessarily heroic. Rather than tell a "bad" story in which the field suffers from the misunderstanding of its compatriots, or a "good" story in which heroic teachers lead students into an enlightened space, I want to critically examine the commonplace of marginalized but noble composition teaching by looking at the teaching of composition as a complex economic enterprise that has almost from its beginnings demanded management as a result of its ubiquity in the ever-expanding American higher education system. The "managerial" is a third term that usefully breaks up the usual dichotomies of teaching/research, marginal/central, and production/consumption that have long circulated through the discourse of composition studies.

This book, in other words, makes the case for a more vigorous materiality in histories of composition studies. Even the most materialist of previous studies of the field, including Bruce Horner's extraordinarily important *Terms of Work for Composition: A Materialist Critique*, understand that work only in terms of writing and teaching writing, without calling attention to writing programs as the workplace of composition. However, before turning to a more specific outline of the historical narrative I will offer, I want to look more closely at that often-troubled term that serves as a framework for this book: the managerial.

## WHAT'S MANAGERIAL ABOUT COMPOSITION STUDIES?

Referring to composition studies as "managerial" has come to be seen as something of an insult, an epithet that shortchanges and dismisses the field of composition studies in general and the work of program administration in particular. More than one professional LISTSERV erupted when an excerpt from Marc Bousquet's *minnesota review* article "Tenured Bosses and Disposable Teachers" appeared in the *Chronicle of Higher Education*, shortly after his collection of the same name, coedited with Tony Scott and Leo Parascondola, was published.[1] In the full article, Bousquet describes "the core self-understanding of the compositionist" to be that of "a managerial intellectual." The "managerial" qualifier seemed to cancel out the "intellectual" label for a number of readers, so that several respondents on the WPA-L complained that Bousquet had overlooked the substantial body of scholarship on administration as intellectual work. Readers on the H-Rhetor list further dismissed Bousquet and those like him as "Gucci Marxists who engage in precisely the cynical disdain—even as they pretend to protect its teachers—that has poisoned English departments for years" (Swearingen) and further accused him of "blaming composition studies for the current labor situation" (Porter).

I don't share the reading of Bousquet's work that would posit him as an enemy of composition studies. Rather, I understand his "disdain" to be not so much for composition studies as a field as for the increasing managerial role of all faculty, as when he suggests, "If rhet-comp is the canary in the mine for the academy more generally, what it tells us is that the professorial jobs of the future are for an increasingly managerial faculty" ("Tenured Bosses"). In fact, his view that all faculty are being required, more and more, to do managerial work is not so far from the view of composition scholar Richard Miller, that all faculty work is bureaucratic work, though they don't reach the same conclusions based on that view. All the same, both Bousquet's writings and the composition community's response to them clearly indicate a default stance in opposition to the very idea of "management." For Bousquet, management is an identity, characterized by "the desire for control" and a general dissatisfaction with the perceived separation from the traditional roles of faculty. For the composition community, whose identity is strongly aligned with teaching and "administration"—not "management"—the affront is more a matter of the perceived separation (on the part of both

Bousquet and the composition community) between management and intellectual work. So while Bousquet describes composition professionals as "managerial intellectuals," he also asserts that they dream of "participating more fully in the intellectual community." And given that Bousquet's opening epigraph from Thomas Frank seems to disparage the idea that management theory has come to be seen as "a perfectly viable replacement for old-fashioned intellectual life," it seems fair to deduce that Bousquet shares this view that would see managerial intellectuals as something other than good "old-fashioned" intellectuals.

However, this dismissing of management as other than intellectual also appears in WPA discourse. Perhaps nothing makes the conflicted status of management within composition studies more clear than the 1998 Council of Writing Program Administrators' "Evaluating the Intellectual Work of Writing Program Administration." The 1990s were a highpoint for critical, political work in composition studies, and so we might read the council's statement as a kind of activist intervention, an effort to redefine administration as intellectual work that should count toward tenure and promotion. Charles Schuster, who drafted a preliminary version of the statement, noted in a 1991 essay that "many of the most famous faculty in rhetoric and composition have, at one time or another in their careers, received some such professional setback [like being denied tenure or promotion]. To list them here would be to write a veritable *Who's Who* of composition" (87). Because their jobs, though better paid, could seem almost as unstable as those of the non-tenure-track instructors they supervised, members of the Council of Writing Program Administrators felt it important to define their work as scholarly and, thus, as supportive of tenure.

In elevating something called "administration" to the level of the scholarly, however, the managerial function is itself downplayed. The document opens with the observation that "administration—including leadership of first-year writing courses, WAC programs, writing centers, and the many other manifestations of writing administration—has for the most part been treated as a management activity that does not produce new knowledge and that neither requires nor demonstrates scholarly expertise and disciplinary knowledge." Drawing from the work of Ernest Boyer and others who have made the case for redefining scholarship, the document's authors align writing program administration with intellectual work, which "produce[s] new knowledge and that . . . requires [and] demonstrates scholarly expertise and disciplinary knowledge," contrasted with "management activity," which does none of these.

But the contrast between managerial activity and disciplinary knowledge in this document points to exactly the separation that I would say Bousquet misses or underplays. Contrary to his assertion, there is no "core self-understanding of the compositionist as a managerial intellectual" ("Tenured Bosses"). Scholarly expertise in composition studies is expertise in pedagogy, rhetoric, or writing theory. That expertise is then applied in administrative settings, thus making writing program administration into intellectual work, since it requires this sort of "disciplinary knowledge" and may produce new knowledge as theories are tested and revised. To suggest that composition specialists are managerial intellectuals is to suggest that they consciously theorize about management, but, as the "Intellectual Work" document makes clear, even the very people involved in administration understand management to be separate from (and implicitly inferior to) the scholarly, disciplinary expertise of writing specialists.

The sticking point for many composition scholars, then, seems to be the word "managerial." Certainly, it has negative connotations for traditional humanist intellectuals, who have tended over the decades to distrust management as, at best, nonintellectual and, at worst, soul-murdering. All the same, it's really a matter of word choice to prefer "administration" over "management." Although management in its current usage is more recent and more aligned with corporate oversight, the function (coordinating the work of other people) is the same. Even so fierce a critic of management as Harry Braverman acknowledges the point that managerial functions predate what he calls monopoly capitalism:

> In the first place, functions of management were brought into being by the very practice of cooperative labor. Even an

assemblage of independently practicing artisans requires co-ordination, if one considers the need for the provision of a workplace and the ordering of processes within it, the centralization of the supply of materials, even the most elementary of scheduling of priorities and assignments. (41)

Raymond Williams further asserts that the distinction between "administration" and "management" is simply one of "politeness," a politeness that follows from ideological distinctions. While "manager" retains a range of meanings from its earlier association with both war (managing of horses and men) and households (*ménager*) to include "applications from sport to business to housekeeping," from the middle of the eighteenth century it was "increasingly used for financial and business activities" (*Keywords* 190). In the twentieth century, as corporate capitalism required greater numbers of people to direct and coordinate the work of disparate parts of private businesses, the term "managers" or "the management" came to be applied as a distinct body from public officials, who were called "civil servants" or referred to as "the bureaucracy" (190). Williams points out that these distinct names continue to apply "even where their actual activities are identical; this follows the received and ideological affected distinction between public and private business" (190). Moreover, "[t]he polite term for semi-public institutions has been the *administration* (though this is also used as a political synonym for *government*)" (190–91).

To recognize that management and administration name the same function in different sites does not, however, negate the leftist critique of class domination and control. For Braverman, "control is indeed the central concept of all management systems, as has been recognized implicitly or explicitly by all theoreticians of management" (47). However, as JoAnne Yates points out in her significant study of office systems, *Control through Communication*, control need not be coercive: "Managerial control—over employees (both workers and other managers), processes, and flows of materials—is the mechanism through which the operations of an organization are coordinated to achieve desired results" (xvi). Managerial control, according to Yates, "is essentially management as we now think of it" and not necessarily coercive (xvi).

Yates's more neutral view of management coincides well with Richard Miller's understanding of academic work as bureaucratic. For Miller, the academy at large—not just composition scholars—composes a kind of bureaucratic unconscious, eschewing managerial control despite the necessity of bureaucratic leadership in order to effect any sort of change. He decries the "willed ignorance about the bureaucratic intricacies of life in the academy," which "is often understood to be both a virtue and a sign of elevated intelligence," and argues that "denying, bemoaning, or critiquing that state of affairs does little to affect prevailing working conditions or to improve the delivery of a meaningful educational experience for undergraduates" (*As If* 3, 9). For Miller, critique is "the easy part." He advocates an embrace of the role of bureaucrat as a role that actually allows one to effect change: "To pursue educational reform is thus to work in an impure space, where intractable material conditions always threaten to expose rhetorics of change as delusional or deliberately deceptive; it is also to insist that bureaucracies don't simply impede change: they are the social instruments that make change possible" (8). For both Yeats and Miller (among others), bureaucracy or management is an enabler, a structure that makes work, and changes in the workplace, possible. Even Tony Scott, in his critique of the bureaucratic status of writing programs, acknowledges that first-year writing programs can "be effectively used to instrumentalize a particular view of literacy and learning" so that "[if] you are a professional in rhetoric and composition who believes that writing portfolios, argumentation, critical pedagogy, or service learning are the way to go . . . , then you can build a program around it" (47).

The problem, however, for Scott is that such bureaucratic control tends to lead to a loss of autonomy for teachers of writing, so that "the work of the average FYC teacher is dictated primarily by local administrative prerogatives" (46). This view echoes Braverman and much of the New Left, who understand managerial control to be always coercive under monopoly capitalism because it always serves the interest of the capitalist rather than the workers, thus alienating laborers from their work:

> *The labor process has become the responsibility of the capitalist.*
> . . . It thus becomes essential for the capitalist that control over

the labor process pass from the hands of the worker into his own. This transition presents itself in history as the *progressive alienation of the process of production* from the worker; to the capitalist, it presents itself as the problem of *management*. (Braverman 39–40; emphases in original)

The problem, in other words, is one of identity: management necessarily identifies with the capitalist rather than with labor.

Given that Bousquet, following Braverman, sees the problem as one of identity, he sees a potential solution in the casting off of the problematic subjectivity: "Just as it is sometimes possible for deans and presidents to shed their administrative subjectivity and return to the labor of the professoriate," he asserts, "perhaps the professional and managerial compositionist can likewise shed the desire for control and embrace the reality of collective agency, even become a part of the academic labor movement" ("Tenured Bosses"). The importance of "collective agency" points to a critical framework based, at least in part, on a humanistic materialism reminiscent of Georg Lukács. The managed, following from the theory of the proletarian standpoint developed in Lukács's *History and Class Consciousness*, share a perspective, one that recognizes their exploitation at the hands of another class. What this theory would mean for composition studies is a field-wide partial standpoint, one that never can fully see what Bousquet calls the "obvious": "From the perspective of the vast majority of university teachers ineligible for tenure, it is obvious that the security and benefits of the 'fortunate' managerial minority are predicated on the insecurity and exploitation of the teaching majority" ("Tenured Bosses").

While holding on to what I see as incontrovertible—that the low wages of non-tenure-track writing faculty amount to economic exploitation—I want to trouble the assumption (certainly standard in Marxist theory) that class in general and management in particular is an *identity*, something that brings with it a fixed social position and perspective. Bousquet, following from the traditional Marxist theories of important scholars like Braverman, understands the managed professional to be a member of an oppressive class unless that identity is explicitly given up and, by extension, the entire university to be corrupted by the domination of this class.

But without falling into the "managerial pragmatism" that Bousquet deplores, one that sees the dominant economic model as determining and absolute, and departing also from Richard Miller's embracing of managerial control as an unproblematic vehicle for change, I would like to suggest that class might instead more usefully be understood as process rather than identity and that economic-related social movement might happen through a network of affiliated actions as well as (or perhaps more effectively than) a collective agent. I take this theory of class-as-process from the groundbreaking work of feminist economic geographers J. K. Gibson-Graham (a pen name shared by two scholars). Bousquet notes that the scholars he refers to as "managerial pragmatists" make the mistake of representing "the economic" as "determining immediately," thus "committing the sort of economic determinism usually ascribed to Marxist thought." In a not unrelated vein, Gibson-Graham identify a strong stance of "capitalocentrism" in most cultural discourse, especially leftist discourse. The problem, for Gibson-Graham, is the equating of "the economic" with "capitalism":

> When we say that most economic discourse is "capitalocentric," we mean that other forms of economy (not to mention noneconomic aspects of social life) are often understood primarily with reference to capitalism: as being fundamentally the same as (or modeled upon) capitalism, or as being deficient or substandard imitations; as being opposite to capitalism; as being the complement of capitalism; as existing in capitalism's space or orbit. (6)

"The economic," according to Gibson-Graham, is not and never has been one; multiple types of economic relations exist alongside capitalist relations—for example, the economics of barter, of gifts, of cooperation. Consequently, to see a singular economic system (read: capitalism) as determining not only is a fundamental mistake but also leads to a pessimism that abandons the hope for change.

If the economic is not one, then neither is class: that is, class is not a singular identity that one possesses and that determines one's view absolutely. Rather, argue Gibson-Graham, class is a process, one that produces, appropriates, and distributes surplus labor: "As an alternative to layered and complex ways of defining class as a social *grouping*, we define class simply as the social *process* of producing and appropriating surplus labor (more commonly known as *exploitation*) and the associated process of surplus labor distribution" (52). By understanding exploitation to be a process rather than a necessary part of a particular identity, and by understanding economics to be plural (in other words, not always based on exploitative relationships), Gibson-Graham hope to enable a greater range of politics, a more open field:

> By producing a knowledge of exploitation as a social process, we hope to contribute to a more self-conscious and self-transformative class subjectivity and to a different politics of class activism and social innovation. Such a politics might not be concerned to eradicate all or even specifically capitalist forms of exploitation but might instead be focused on transforming the extent, type, and conditions of exploitation in particular settings, or on changing its emotional components or its social effects. It might not necessarily invoke the emancipatory agency of a mass collective subject unified around a set of shared "interests" but could arise out of momentary and partial identifications between subjects constituted at the intersection of very different class and nonclass processes and positions. (53–54)

If, following from Gibson-Graham, we understand that a person acting in a managerial role is not by definition a member of an exploiting class—although that person may by default be contributing to an exploitative class process—then it becomes possible to see writing programs as sites of class struggle, as sites "focused on transforming the extent, type, and conditions of exploitation in particular settings."[2]

To manage, then, is not necessarily to exploit, though it may by default contribute to exploitation when the work of management is not critically examined. What seems essential, then, is not to get rid of the managerial function: all complex organizations, which certainly include writing programs, depend on some sort of leadership. What *is* essential is that the effects of that work are always examined, that we do not dismiss as unnecessary what Richard Miller regards as the "easy part" of critique. Critical questions need to be asked: When does leadership become exploitation? How can a person in a managerial position work *with* the people being managed rather than take advantage of them?

The field of composition studies, in my view, does not need to defend itself against the "managerial" epithet. Rather, those in the field need indeed to act as "managerial intellectuals," but managerial intellectuals of a particular kind. During the decade of the 1990s, while composition studies itself was becoming increasingly politicized, critical management studies was emerging within the discipline of management. Although some humanists have suggested that this group is a kind of cover-up for the necessarily exploitative work of management, those involved in this movement understand their work differently. According to the Critical Management area on the Academy of Management website:

> The Critical Management Studies Interest Group serves as a forum within the Academy for the expression of views critical of established management practices and the established social order. Our premise is that structural features of contemporary society, such as the profit imperative, patriarchy, racial inequality, and ecological irresponsibility[,] often turn organizations into instruments of domination and exploitation. Driven by a shared desire to change this situation, we aim in our research, teaching, and practice to develop critical interpretations of management and society and to generate radical alternatives. Our critique seeks to connect the practical shortcomings in management and individual managers to the demands of a socially divisive and ecologically destructive system within which managers work. (Critical Management)

Surely, these are worthy goals for composition studies as well: to "develop critical interpretations of [writing program] management . . . and to generate radical alternatives." A preliminary step toward this goal, it seems to me, is to understand the ways in which the field's emergence has been inextricably tied to a managerial imperative.

## HISTORICIZING THE MANAGERIAL
## OF COMPOSITION STUDIES

This book, then, makes a case for understanding the history of the field of composition studies as the history of the increasing importance of managers of the teaching of writing. It opens with a chapter that critically analyzes the emergence of writing programs in the first half of the twentieth century. Drawing from a range of historical documents related to both composition teaching and office work, I set up an analogy between the teaching of required college writing and the secretarial work of what may be assumed to be routinized writing in order to highlight the ways that hierarchies and divisions of labor have become attached to cultural ideologies about language use. This chapter demonstrates that the current configurations of writing programs are analogous to the configurations of the corporate workplace; that divisions of labor emerged, as they emerged in corporations, to make work more efficient; and that when one level of work came to be associated with routine and correctness, then it came to be associated with women and with whiteness.

With the emergence of writing programs, a distinct role became increasingly prominent, that of the director of what was then commonly known as freshman English. Chapters 2 through 4 each take one prominent scholar/director as a kind of case study to base a farther-ranging examination of the field at three significant junctures: the founding of the Conference on College Composition and Communication (CCCC) in 1949, the founding of the Council of Writing Program Administrators in 1977, and the so-called social turn of the field in the 1990s.

Chapter 2 thus begins with George Wykoff, a founding member of the CCCC and an early advocate of professionalization. The increase in college enrollments after World War II led to ever-growing demands on these directors, resulting in the founding of a professional organization to better address their needs. Texts connected with the founding of the CCCC—the professional organization for composition specialists—and with the emergence of the dominant process paradigm for teaching composition tend to figure composition teachers as confused masses in need of professional management. The second chapter uses these documents to show that in addition to being a revolution in teaching, the professionalizing of composition has been a revolution in the management of teaching writing, a revolution that parallels the so-called managerial revolution in American business.

The third chapter examines more fully this managerial revolution in the teaching of writing in the context of an administratively heavy "multiversity." In addition to tracing the continued growth of the corporate university and proliferating writing programs (including basic writing programs, writing-across-the-curriculum programs, and the like), I draw from early bulletins of the Council of Writing Program Administrators to trace the exigencies that prompted that organization's founding. Kenneth Bruffee, an early president of the organization and editor of its journal, serves as the instructive basis of my investigation. Given that the CCCC was originally designed to meet the needs of directors of freshman English, I consider how the CCCC had changed and how the Council of Writing Program Administrators was responding to new developments in a managed university that gave increasing value to programmatic development.

The fourth and final chapter examines the "social turn" in composition studies during the 1990s, which brought new attention to collaborative forms of pedagogy and ideological forms of criticism. It is often figured as inherently progressive. I argue that these social pedagogies mirror trends in management, such as Total Quality Management, which similarly advocate a democratic, collaborative organization of the workplace. I draw especially from the work of James Berlin as an important case study of this social turn and from studies of Total Quality Management to demonstrate that appeals to the inherent "democratic" work of teaching may also function as emotional incentives to work with more commitment, even if that commitment is not rewarded with better working conditions.

To conclude, I call for the field of composition studies to bring a critical, curious, and even skeptical attention to writing program administration, allowing for not just the "intellectual work of administration" (as called for in the council document "Evaluating the Intellectual Work of Writing Program Administrators") but for an "operative reason" (rather than instrumental reason) that will never take any managerial strategy as the final word on the teaching of writing.[3]

# 1

## The Emergence of Writing Programs and the Cultural Work of Composition Teaching

A 1907 ADVERTISEMENT for the Edison dictating machine provides a striking illustration of the arrangement of writing labor in the emergent corporate workplace.[1] On the left, a suited man reclines in his office chair, one hand leisurely dropped to his side, the other holding a dictating machine's speaking tube in front of his mouth. On the right, a demurely dressed woman outfitted with earphones sits up straight at her desk, her hands on the typewriter before her, transcribing the dictated words. The copy, set off in a circle between the two figures, reads: "FROM BRAIN TO TYPE." Physically separating the man and the woman in the advertisement, the large, bold-faced words offer a telling representation and interpretation of the corporate workplace as it was developing around the turn of the century. The written word was—and continues to be—deployed in this setting to coordinate and manage the work of the various parts of the hierarchically organized corporate body. So voluminous and essential was the production of writing in the modern corporation that this work itself necessitated a division between conceptual and mechanical labor. Already in the early years of this century, as the Edison advertisement suggests, white, native-born men assumed control over the mental work of producing words, while white, native-born women were rapidly becoming the workers of choice to fix the words of the masculine brain into print.

As secretarial work was becoming increasingly associated with white women in the first half of the twentieth century, so was the work of teaching required writing in American universities.[2] By 1929, women taught 42 percent of all courses in first-year English offered at midwestern and western colleges—where, in contrast to eastern and southern colleges, coeducation was the norm—and 36 percent of those offered in the entire United States, while making up only 29 percent of the total faculty in American colleges and universities and holding only 4 percent of the full professorships in coeducational institutions (Taylor 559–60; Carnegie Commission 113; Lonn 5). Given the overwhelming bias against women faculty at the time—as Eileen Schell has pointed out, many administrators answering a 1929 survey on freshman English were vehement in their insistence that no women taught in their departments—the number of women teaching composition was quite high (*Gypsy Academics* 32). The course in required writing itself, as Susan Miller has argued, emerged at least in part to prepare students for the demands of a curriculum based upon writing, writing that was used to manage and examine the growing student body.[3] Writing, in other words, functioned as a management tool in the corporate workplace and in the university classroom, and women increasingly came to be employed in both settings to carry out the work of seeing words into material form.

The Edison commercial system, conducted with the business phonograph.
Courtesy of Hagley Museum and Library, Wilmington, Delaware.

In drawing this analogy between the workplace pictured in the Edison advertisement and the workplace in which writing is taught—

that is, college and university writing programs—I wish to suggest that a further exploration of this analogy might provide what Fredric Jameson has called a "cognitive mapping" of some of the material and ideological networks from which writing programs emerged. Cognitive mapping offers "a spatial analysis of culture," an interpretation of the ways in which material conditions generate "a type of space unique" to those conditions ("Cognitive" 348). A number of scholars, most notably Richard Ohmann, have produced important critical analyses of the corporate economy and its impact on departments of English. Scholars like Ohmann, however, focus primarily on the ways in which the teaching of English is *determined* by capitalist interests and thus have little to say about the complex networks of economic and cultural discourses that make up English departments in general and writing programs in particular. The Edison advertisement hints at some of these discursive networks: the division between the thinking white man and the typing white woman are not merely economic (an employer/employee relationship) but ideological and affective (so that it is the man, not the woman, who is linked to "brain"). I will argue that this corporate dividing practice is also at work in writing programs, which have been overdetermined by economic contingencies, managerial logics, and ideologies of gender and race. Understanding the convergence of these factors should provide insight into the complicated dynamics of this workplace—a workplace that has come under scrutiny not only in composition studies (Schell, *Gypsy Academics*; Crowley, *Composition*) but also in English studies more generally (Bérubé; Bousquet, *How the University Works*).

One strand within my argument—the tendency toward the feminization of composition teaching within writing programs—has been noted by many scholars (see Holbrook; Susan Miller; Schell, "Cost"; Connors, "Rhetoric"; Enos). As Sue Ellen Holbrook, drawing upon a large body of scholarship that documents gendered divisions of labor, explains, feminized occupations are those that tend to disproportionately employ women and also provide less pay and prestige (202). Scholars in composition studies have begun to speak out against the contingent status and inferior pay visited upon so many composition teachers. While the issue of labor has received increasing attention (the 1998 CCCC, for example, included work-shops on collective bargaining and on improving the status of non-tenure-track faculty), the material circumstances and ideological underpinnings that have given rise to the current workplace arrangement of that labor have rarely been scrutinized. Robert Connors, in what has become a commonplace understanding in the field of composition studies, attributes the "underclass" status of composition teachers to their association with teaching in departments that give priority to research ("Rhetoric"). This line of reasoning, however, does not account for the renewed valorization of teaching that arose at places like Harvard during the very time that required composition courses were being established. Schell has persuasively linked the ideologies of feminine nurturing and care to many women's willingness to remain in positions of contingent, service-oriented employment. While the ideology of feminine care circulates and exerts immense power in the current configuration of composition teaching, I am interested in understanding the conditions that made the present configuration possible and, moreover, made possible the employment of women to teach college writing despite a tendency—especially pronounced around the turn of the century—toward seeing writing as a masculine activity (see Brody; Townsend). Moreover, the ideology that links women with teaching fails to account for the prevalence of white women and the scarcity of women of color among composition teachers (see Logan, "'When'").

What is missing in most accounts of the feminization of composition teaching, and in the history of composition more generally, is the emergence of writing programs—the emergence, that is, of the contemporary configuration of the workplace in which the teaching of composition is done. Indeed, the emergence of writing programs, an emergence that frames the very conditions of possibility of the contemporary study of composition, is a looming hole in the field's history. Robin Varnum has observed that the period that gave rise to writing programs is one of the most widely neglected eras in composition's history: "The sixty years between roughly 1900 and 1960 have been characterized as a period of stagnation in the history of composition and as a period in which 'current-traditional' rhetoric

. . . operated as a monolithic and increasingly obstructive paradigm" (39). For example, although James Berlin in *Rhetoric and Reality* does acknowledge that "organized freshman writing programs" began to emerge from 1920 to 1940, in linking these programs with current-traditional rhetoric, he marginalizes writing programs as a development largely at odds with the privileged story of social-epistemic rhetoric (65). My contention, however, is that the emergence of writing programs represents a pivotal development in composition's history and deserves far greater attention than it has yet received.

This chapter will map out two simultaneous and mutually reinforcing phenomena: first, the material conditions that have given rise to hierarchically arranged writing programs, and second, the attendant cultural values that have made possible the feminization as well as the racialization of composition teaching and that stratify the workplace. The Edison advertisement, representing as it does a workplace in which writing is separated into the conceptual labor of dictating words and the mechanical labor of taking dictation, will serve as a controlling image for this investigation. In addition to graphically illustrating a workplace divided by gender-coded writing duties, it suggests additional values associated with gender and writing. The woman in the advertisement takes up little space at her desk; her body is carefully controlled both through her upright posture and her high-necked, ankle-length dress. She is, clearly, a vivid image of propriety, signifying links between femininity, whiteness, writing, and morality. At the same time that she signifies feminine lack (as opposed to a masculine brain), she simultaneously signifies white privilege—an upright woman who can be trusted with the white man's words.

By paying attention to the ideological coding of composition teaching while describing the emergence of writing programs, moreover, I want to firmly establish the inextricable connection between program administration and the teaching of writing. The teaching of writing, as we know it, is a highly managed enterprise. To address the emergence of writing programs without attention to the people who are employed to teach writing is to create a mere abstraction. And to address the teaching of writing, as has traditionally been done in rhetoric and composition studies, without attention to the managed nature of that work is to alienate teaching labor from the work of rhetoric and composition studies.

My argument is that the current configurations of writing programs are analogous to the configurations of the corporate workplace; that divisions of labor emerged, as they emerged in corporations, to make work more efficient; and that when one level of work came to be associated with routine and correctness, then it came to be associated with white women, even as the work of supervision remained primarily the province of white men. In other words, writing programs emerged as divisions of labor that are ideologically coded and maintained through the circulation of dominant cultural values. It is this simultaneous dividing and coding that has made possible the feminization and the attendant racialization of composition teaching. At stake in this argument is an understanding of both the material conditions that have produced the current configurations of composition teaching within the workplace of writing programs and the cultural values that circulate and are reproduced by way of these configurations. In order to clarify my argument, I want to separate out three strands that converge in the emergence of writing programs and that are illustrated in the Edison advertisement. Although I separate them here, these strands are ultimately overlapping and inseparable: the order in which I present them is not meant to imply a chronological order of causation. Rather, what I hope to show is (1) writing programs emerged as a result of a division of labor necessitated by the ubiquity and central importance of required writing—not, as some scholars have suggested, by the "marginalization" of writing; (2) this division increasingly was formed along lines familiar in the capitalist workplace—the division between head and hands, intellectual work and mechanical work; and (3) the "mechanical" aspects of English were associated with women, particularly white women, while the creative, "executive" aspects were associated with white men.

## DIVIDING THE LABOR OF WRITING

Central to my argument is an understanding of writing programs as divisions of labor that resulted not from the marginalization of writing or of teaching but from the essential function of writing in the university curriculum. Although some historians of composition, like John Brereton, refer to A. S. Hill of Harvard as the creator of the "first modern composition program," writing programs did not emerge simultaneously with the required course in composition (Introduction 8). Rather, the division of labor that made writing programs possible emerged as universities expanded and enrollments swelled with the advent of corporate capitalism. Writing programs, in other words, were made possible not by the devaluing of student writing in the university but by its central function in an institution that depended on writing as a tool for surveillance and assessment.

The division of writing labor illustrated in the Edison advertisement—the division between the thinking of words and the transcribing of words—was made necessary by the proliferation of writing that circulated in the new corporate workplace, a proliferation that emerged simultaneously with the accumulation of student writing in departments of English and, more generally, in the university as a whole. In both cases, the written word was deployed to manage the ever-growing groups of people that were being brought together in expanding corporations and universities. Formal written communication became "the principal tool of managerial control" in larger businesses, a development chronicled in JoAnne Yates's *Control through Communication* (xvi). At the same time, the shift from recitation to written examinations in American universities emerged as a way to sort students and exert control over intellectual production (see Bledstein; S. Miller). The written word, in short, functioned in corporations and universities as a prominent tool for the enforcement of discipline in the new phase of capitalist expansion.

The explosion in the use of writing in American businesses accompanied a new philosophy of management that developed in the wake of corporate expansion. This philosophy, known as systematic or scientific management, replaced "ad hoc managerial methods," based upon informal and largely oral communication, with "rational and impersonal systems" that were meant to eliminate personal idiosyncrasies and inefficiency (Yates 1). In this new phase of capitalist development, "networks of communication up, down, and across hierarchies" were increasingly deployed to hold corporations together and to systematize the work throughout the firm, requiring that "employees at all levels read and write countless memoranda, letters, and reports" (xv). The demands of producing and storing this written material made new divisions of labor necessary (Strom 26, 173). A single person could no longer be expected to manage the work of his subordinates *and* physically produce the documents that made this management possible. The practice of scientific management thus made writing necessary as a disciplinary tool in the corporate workplace—as a method for organizing and supervising work—while it also rationalized a division of labor for the efficient production of that writing. The persons in charge of the physical production of written communication—stenographers, typists, secretaries—were not the people in charge of conceptualizing and enforcing forms of workplace control.

The labor occasioned by an accumulation of paper also brought on calls for a better division of labor in the teaching of English. In 1892, a special committee formed by the Harvard Board of Overseers reported that a total of "over 6,000" compositions were being read by instructors in the required freshman course each semester, and, further, "the number of separate exercises handed in to all the instructors of the English Department is estimated at thirty-eight thousand" (Adams, Godkin, and Quincy 76). In addition to taking advantage of the sheer shock value of these numbers, the committee reported these statistics as ample evidence of the veracity of their opening statement:

> Few persons not intimately connected . . . with the existing Department of Rhetoric and English Composition . . . have any conception of either the amount or nature of the work now done by the instructors in that department. In quantity this work is calculated to excite dismay; while the performance of it involves not only unremitted industry, but mental drudgery of the most exhausting nature. (75)

The quantification of work ("In quantity this work is calculated to excite dismay") and the discourse of fatigue ("mental drudgery of the most exhausting nature") were central concerns in the late-nineteenth- and early-twentieth-century efforts to make a science of work (see Rabinbach 45–68). If the quantity of work was so great as to produce exhaustion in the worker, then work must be in some way rearranged in order to maintain efficient production. The creation of more finely drawn divisions of labor was a common strategy for arranging work so that it could be, in principle, carried out more efficiently (see Foucault, *Discipline* 141–49). Because the "principles of systematic management [had] entered public discourse early in the twentieth century," words and concepts such as "system" and "efficiency" would have been circulating already as this report was written in the last decade of the nineteenth century (Yates 15).[4] Moreover, because Charles Francis Adams, one of the three members of the Harvard committee, was chairman of the Massachusetts Railroad Commission and a prominent expert on railroad management, he may have directly imported systematic management ideas into the Harvard reports (Chandler 139). As a railroad expert, Adams would have been involved in early uses of systematic/scientific management because, as Yates explains, "the railroads were important early innovators in managerial theory and practice, pioneering in the use of formal internal communication for control" (4).

Whether the ideas of systematic management were employed consciously or unconsciously, articulating the correct divisions of labor in the teaching of English was clearly the burden of the committee's report. The committee observed that a division of labor had already occurred within the required freshman course, as one of the instructors reported: "In 1890–91, the lecture-room provided for the Freshmen was so crowded that a division of the class had to be made. It was thought that perhaps some relief from the burden of the unprepared might be obtained by sending them off to be lectured to separately" (qtd. in Adams, Godkin, and Quincy 76). Apparently, the committee wished to avoid divisions of labor within the college itself; the appearance of a division of labor among instructors of freshman composition led the committee to call for a better division of labor between the secondary schools and the university. The members of the committee determined that "a large amount of work not properly belonging to it was . . . imposed on the College" (77) and expressed both ideological and economic objections to this work:

> The College . . . instead of being what its name implies,—a seminary of higher education,—becomes . . . a mere academy, the instructors in which are subjected to the drudgery of teaching the elements. . . . At present a large corps of teachers have to be engaged and paid from the College treasury to do that which should have been done before the student presented himself for admission. (96)

The work of "teaching the elements" was considered inappropriate because such learning was for children, not for Harvard men. Moreover, because this course required "a large corps of teachers," it represented a considerable expense for the university. Thus, the ideology of what constituted appropriate masculine activities and the economics of employing a large number of instructors worked together to convince the committee that "the work of theme writing ought to be pronounced a part of the elementary training, and as such relegated to the preparatory schools" (96).

The committee's recommendation echoed an argument put forth some twenty years previous by A. S. Hill, the originator of the required composition course at Harvard. Although he considered composition to be a central feature of the college curriculum, Hill nonetheless felt that the teaching of certain aspects of English should be confined to the secondary schools: "For [the college] to teach bearded men the rudiments of their native tongue would be almost as absurd as to teach them the alphabet or the multiplication table. Those who call for 'more English' in the colleges should cry aloud and spare not till more and better English is taught in the schools" (51). Rudimentary skills in English, according to Hill, were childish acquisitions, hardly appropriate for teaching to "bearded men." All the same, when Hill first began teaching at Harvard, the enrollment was sufficiently small to make it possible to attend to students of various ability levels. Even in 1884, one year before the required course was moved from the sophomore to the freshman year, Hill taught this course with the help of only one assistant (Brown 29). By 1890, however, as we have seen, the number of students taking the required freshman course was sufficiently large that a division of the class, and a division in the labor of the instructors, became necessary. Further, as we have also seen, the appearance of this division of labor led to renewed calls for reform of the secondary school curriculum, a reform that would, presumably, make the division of labor within the college unnecessary.

The desire not only to divide the labor of writing but also to spatialize and clarify that division by keeping one sort of labor in the high school and another sort in the college continued into the twentieth century (and, indeed, continues today in media representations of high schools that "are not doing their jobs"). Writing in 1923, J. R. Rutland, a professor of English at Alabama Polytechnic Institute (now Auburn University), joined Hill and the members of the Harvard committee in calling for "a better division of labor between the high school and college" (2). Rutland hoped for this institutional division of labor despite his own presentation of evidence that divisions were proliferating within college English departments. Having conducted a survey that inquired into the administration of freshman English at forty American colleges and universities, he found two broad tendencies in dividing the labor of teaching writing within the college itself. One tendency, which the Harvard committee had already observed as early as 1892, was toward the formation of separate need-based sections of composition: "Those students who are found deficient are put into sub-Freshman English for which there is no credit, as in the universities of Wisconsin and Illinois; or are placed in separate sections so that their short-comings may receive special attention, as at Purdue" (3). Another tendency was toward complete separation of the teaching of composition from the teaching of literature; many technical schools, Rutland noted, were tending "toward the separation of faculties of composition and rhetoric" (5). These two kinds of division, which were already fairly well established in 1923, characterize the modern writing program: the faculty of the writing program tends to be separate from the faculty in literature, and the program itself tends to be divided into various levels of courses appropriate for differently prepared students.

Rutland clearly disapproved of the tendency toward dividing the labor of teaching composition from the labor of teaching literature. Yet (for reasons I will explore in the next section) by the next decade, this practice seems to have been so commonplace that the alternative preferred by the Harvard committee and Rutland—avoiding a division of labor within the university by articulating a better division of labor between high schools and colleges—seems to have lost its appeal. In an infamous attack on required composition published in 1939, Oscar James Campbell rails against the de facto segregation of faculty yet considers it unavoidable: "I know of large departments in which no one has been promoted from an instructorship [in the teaching of composition] to an assistant professorship [in the teaching of literature] for over ten years. . . . This process is natural—yes, inevitable—because the work of Freshman English does not fit him for the teaching of literature" (182). Campbell's proposed solution to the problem of a separate, debased composition faculty was to argue for the abolition of freshman composition; writing, he felt, was more effectively taught within subject areas. This argument for a prototypical writing-across-the-curriculum program represents a significant shift from the earlier calls for a better division of labor between high schools and colleges. While Campbell, like the Harvard committee before him, objected to the appearance of divisions of labor within the English department, his solution was simply to dissolve the division rather than to shift it outside of the university.

Although Campbell's dismal view of writing instruction, which borrows from the language of natural selection, may seem familiar, it was by no means monolithic. In the same year that Campbell published his attack, more positive defenses of the separation of faculties appeared. Blanche Colton Williams, for example, divided the work of teaching English into three distinct job descriptions: the teacher of language, the teacher of literature, and the teacher of composition. She in fact argued against the very idea that composition teachers should "be promoted" to the teaching of literature. Any teacher who wished for this procedure "is not one essentially of composition, or does not rate correctly its importance" (409). She continued: "Of the genus 'English professor,' the composition teacher is a distinct species. His intention and desire are to help students express themselves in written English and through expression to live more largely in at least cubical dimensions" (409). Although her description of the place of composition teachers also draws upon biological classifications, she considered the status of the composition teacher to be, in principle, equal to that of the teacher of literature or language. While George Wykoff, who would become a central figure in the founding of the CCCC, acknowledged with Campbell that composition teachers are often an unhappy group, he argued that a person might reasonably choose composition teaching as a career if the universities were to provide better training and incentives. Like both Campbell and Williams, Wykoff did not challenge the necessity of separating the work of the composition faculty from that of the literature faculty. By 1939, then, the existence of a separate writing program composed of faculty separate from the faculty in literature was an established, if sometimes still contested, phenomenon.

What should be clear from this account is that writing programs began to form as a result of divisions of labor, prompted by the corporate logic of scientific management, in order to make the teaching of writing more efficient. Further, just as the division of the physical production of written documents in the corporate workplace resulted not from a loss of importance in those documents but rather from the need to render their production more efficient and less costly, so does the division of the teaching of writing from the rest of the English department represent an effort to make that work more efficient and, through the classification of that teaching as entry-level work, less costly. Dividing the teaching of writing from the teaching of literature, in other words, represents a decision based not on a devaluing of writing but on economic and managerial logics. That is not to say that the work is not then looked down upon by those who aspire for a more stable, more lucrative position: what prospective business executive, after all, would welcome an opportunity to begin work in a firm as a typist? It is, rather, to suggest that the division of labor, rather than simply the work or subject itself, contributes to the hierarchical arrangement of English departments. It is the division of labor that makes possible the dismal state of affairs to which Campbell alludes: composition teaching often was not, as Williams more optimistically suggests, rewarded in the same way as the teaching of literature. Just as secretarial work became more clearly separated from managerial work and thus promised little possibility of promotion into those ranks, so did composition teaching, in the process of becoming more clearly separated from literature teaching, come to be associated with non-tenure-track positions.

### THE MECHANIZATION OF WRITING

In the Edison advertisement, the division of writing labor is represented as a division between mental labor and a version of labor somewhere between manual and mental: the man uses his brain as he gives dictation, while the woman uses her hands to type the dictated words. More precisely, the division is between the ability to form concepts and the ability to reproduce those concepts mechanically through the intervention of a series of machines (in this case, the dictating machine and the typewriter). In this section, I will trace the ideological lines along which the writing program came to be separated from the English department in order to observe the struggle between definitions of writing as, on the one hand, intellectual work and, on the other hand, mechanical work. The point of this analysis is to demonstrate the ways in which ideologies of writing support the economic and managerial logic of divisions of labor in writing programs.

An examination of the division of labor that emerged in the teaching of English makes clear that the required course in composition was not, at first, conceived to be a course in mechanical correctness. Although, as Robert Connors has shown in his "Mechanical Correctness as a Focus in Composition Instruction," an obsession with correctness circulated in nineteenth-century America, the earliest courses in college composition were not meant to be courses in the mechanics of English. Rather, Hill and his contemporaries—including Michigan's Fred Newton Scott—were much more concerned with the often nebulous category of style. LeBaron Briggs, one of Hill's assistants and later the Boylston Professor of Rhetoric at Harvard, hoped that composition students might acquire "the style of a straightforward gentleman" (61). Further, the acquisition of style was considered a way of developing individuality, as Walter Rollo Brown described it: "[Hill and his associates] trained men to look at the world with their own eyes, and to write directly and honestly about what they saw, without regard for the traditional ways of looking at things" (33). Kathryn T. Flannery has demonstrated, moreover, that the concept of style functioned "as an important link" between the teaching of composition and the teaching of literature: the teaching of English, whether composition or literature, was, primarily, the teaching of style (122; see also 101–13). Scott, who is generally considered to be a forefather of social-epistemic rhetoric, was an especially vocal advocate for the teaching of style, arguing "for the importance of seeing composition, rhetoric, and literary study as intertwined" (Flannery 122).

Those who called for a better division of labor between the secondary school and the college were, as I have argued, seeking to render the teaching of writing more efficient and, at the same time, to maintain a distinctive conception of college English. The Harvard committee hoped to guard the development of style and independent manliness as work for the college alone by distinguishing it—dividing it—from the work of teaching the "rudiments" of writing:

> It is the University, not the Preparatory School, which has to do with "style" and "individuality," "Mass, Coherence and Form," with, in a word, that much abused and misused branch of study known in educational parlance as "Rhetoric." The province of the preparatory schools is to train the scholar . . . in what can only be described as the elements and rudiments of written expression,—they should teach facile, clear penmanship, correct spelling, simple grammatical construction, and neat, workmanlike, mechanical execution. (Adams, Godkin, and Nutter 123)

The teaching of style, which the committee associated with the teaching of rhetoric, was the work of the university; the teaching of the "mechanical execution" of writing belonged in the secondary schools. Further, just as the committee hoped that students would develop "workmanlike" writing before coming to college, so they had no qualms about describing the teaching of these skills as work-manlike. The committee frankly expected precollegiate schooling to be hard, uninspiring work. Teaching "the elements and rudiments of written expression," they declared, "demands steady, daily drill, and drudgery of a kind most wearisome. Its purpose and aim are not ambitious,—its work is not inspiring;—no more ambitious and no more inspiring than the similar elementary drill in the musical scales, or the mixing of colors and drawing of straight lines" (123). The secondary school teacher of writing should not seek to inspire, should not seek to cultivate the student's intellectual capacities. Instead, the teacher should be content with the wearying labor of daily, elementary drill.[5] If done properly, the secondary school teacher's labor would then provide the college teacher with the freedom to pursue the intellectual and individual work of teaching style.

Although the desire to dissociate the college composition course from mechanical work in order to more decidedly associate it with intellectual work was expressed differently on different campuses, it long remained a central concern in the debates over the proper division of labor. Rutland, for example, drawing from his survey of forty American colleges and universities, reported that "most English teachers still look upon the course [in freshman English] as an introduction to intellectual culture" (4). In elaborating the purpose of this course, Rutland distinguishes between "mental" work and mere training in writing: "The aim is to broaden the student's mental horizon, not simply to train him to write" (4). This introduction to "intellectual culture" came in various forms: though literary study was certainly the most common, Rutland also identified a composition course allied with political science and another that served as an introduction to "the history of civilization" as particularly innovative methods of "helping [the student] toward culture" (4).

At the same time that the responses to his survey convinced Rutland that most colleges continued to regard the composition course as a site for intellectual work, they also served to remind him that this ideal was rarely upheld in practice, that often the course was devoted to mechanical, rather than conceptual, matters. He lamented that much of what was being taught in the freshman course was "often largely secondary in kind and quality" (1) and blamed the "narrowing aim of Freshman English" not merely on the preparation of the students but also on "this age of business and invention," which is "somewhat skeptical of the value of culture" (4). He noted that many technical schools, in particular, were tending "to eliminate literature from Freshman English" (5). Rutland voiced a concern that this division of labor—separating the teaching of composition completely from the teaching of literature, which represented for him a division between mechanical and conceptual labor—might not be in the best interest of education. Though he was willing to concede that "it may be wise, as a matter of administration, to separate the composition course from the literature course," he questioned whether it is "wise, as a matter of education, to abandon the literary element of the Freshman course until a better way of putting Freshman into vital connection with vigorous thinking and humane culture has been devised and adopted" (5). This question suggests a distrust of the encroachment of the logic of business on education, an uneasiness with valuing matters of administration—which would suggest the rationality of dividing the labor of teaching writing into conceptual and mechanical work—over matters of education.

Despite his apparent ambivalence toward the values of the corporate world, Rutland appropriated the language of scientific management to argue against the separation of teachers of composition and literature, maintaining that such an arrangement "throws an excessive burden on the composition instructor" and represents "a specious efficiency" (6, 9). The language of scientific management circulated so widely during this period that it operated as a powerful constraint on the possibilities of argument. Though he distrusted corporate values, Rutland nonetheless lived in a world shaped by those values. Consequently, he argued not for an abandonment of efficiency but for a better articulation between means and ends as a way of achieving efficiency:

> After all, the wider success of Freshman English depends upon its aim as well as upon the efficiency with which the aim is accomplished. If the purpose is simply to teach correct, effective sentences, well-advanced matriculates should be excused

so that the faculty may concentrate upon the deficient and the separation of faculties of composition and literature is worth consideration. If, on the contrary, the aim is also to encourage a catholicity of interests and to develop literary appreciation, to give the bright boy something in Freshman English which he needs and wants, the classification of new students in carefully graded sections will be most helpful, and the separation of faculties of composition and literature would be a hindrance. The fact that most boys can never be taught to write is no sufficient reason for making Freshman English a course in sentence making or logical arrangement. (9)

Rutland argued that "carefully graded sections" of composition provide a better means toward ensuring that students will continue to receive intellectual training in composition. "Carefully graded sections" were, in fact, a common strategy and remain a familiar characteristic of writing programs, as noted in the previous section. Hierarchically arranged writing programs allowed the supposedly nonintellectual work of mechanical correctness to enter the university in an enclosed space. Syracuse University, for example, offered students three semesters of writing instruction. Writing in 1924, Norman J. Whitney reported that students with the highest placement test scores were assigned only the third semester course, which was devoted to the writing of themes in response to literature. The first semester course, in contrast, involved no theme writing; it was "largely a course in sentences" and included weekly "drill work" (487). The second semester course was devoted primarily to theme writing and to developing in students a "sense of his own responsibility for improvement and passing" (486). One of the methods toward this end was the indication of errors on themes "according to the '*Century Handbook* method,'" which, presumably, required students to go to the handbook to identify and subsequently correct any errors the instructor had marked (486). The second semester course functioned as a kind of transition between the teaching of mechanical correctness and the teaching of individuality, between mechanical work and fully realized intellectual work.

In addition to being divided from the rest of the English department, then, the writing program tends to be divided from within: different kinds of labor are demanded of both teacher and student in hierarchically arranged sections. The course at the top point of the hierarchy, being devoted to literary study and thus to conceptual labor, could be taught by literature faculty (which explains Rutland's preference for the system of graded sections). The course at the bottom of the hierarchy, however, was a course in mechanical drill, a system of instruction that tended to be (and continues to be) conceived of as pre-intellectual and vilified as "pre-college." Again, these divisions represent ideologically coded divisions in labor: in order to efficiently teach intellectual production, the writing program separates out the work of teaching mechanical production. The hierarchically arranged writing program represents a concession on the college's part: rather than simply continuing to insist that the labor of teaching mechanical correctness belongs in the secondary school, the college has agreed to take on that work. However, the position of the course in "sentences" or "mere training in writing" at the bottom of a hierarchy of writing courses continues to signal its separation from the intellectual labor of composing themes and studying literature. While Rutland hoped that the practice of establishing graded sections of composition would forestall the separation of composition faculty from literature faculty, more often these two divisions emerged simultaneously (as evidenced by Wykoff's program at Purdue). In short, writing programs tended to divide the labor of teaching writing not only to make that teaching more efficient and more economical but at the same time to distinguish the teaching of the mechanics of English from the conceptual work of English.

## THE FEMINIZATION AND RACIALIZATION
## OF MECHANICAL CORRECTNESS

In addition to offering the promise of "efficiency," then, the divisions of labor that form writing programs also reinforce and are maintained through cultural ideologies and deep-seated cultural values: insofar as required writing is identified with "mechanical" correctness, it is regarded as menial labor. The teaching of literature—even the teaching of writing about literature—is identified as intellectual work and seen as more prestigious. In this section, I will pursue the way in which these ideological codings of mechanical versus intellectual labor further participate in the circulation of cultural value through their association with gendered and racialized ideologies. The feminization of composition teaching, I will argue, signals a complex intersection of cultural values, a process that tends to relegate women to the lowest levels of the academic hierarchy while simultaneously elevating the primarily white, native-born teachers as keepers of correctness and racial propriety.

In the previous sections, I demonstrated the process by which the required course in freshman English, an intended site for the cultivation of individual and masculine style in the post–Civil War college (see Bledstein; Townsend), became increasingly associated with routine, nonconceptual work as it came to be part of a writing program that was separate from the rest of the English department. At the same time, women were more frequently being employed to teach required writing. Stith Thompson of Indiana University, for example, noted this tendency in 1930: "Women instructors . . . do often seem to be willing to settle down to a life of efficient Freshman teaching without any idea of going farther in their academic career" (555).

The divisions of labor that constitute writing programs suggest both economic and ideological explanations for this process of feminization—the process, to be more precise, of describing work that tends not to lead to career advancement as particularly suitable for women. Economic factors have certainly played a determining role. The gendered division of labor, which the Edison advertisement portrays so clearly, tended to dictate that men would occupy better paying, more prestigious positions in corporations. Although feminized professions may be understood to be particularly suited to women, this understanding does not necessarily preclude men from seeking employment in these professions. (Men may, however, pay a psychic cost for involvement in work that has been feminized.) What feminization does tend to preclude is the possibility of women's seeking employment in jobs that have not been designated as appropriate to women—jobs that tend to offer better pay and more stability. Feminization also tends to keep pay low in jobs that have come to be associated with women. The teaching of required writing had become, in the process of being divided from the English department in the name of efficiency, sometimes an entry-level position, more frequently in recent decades a position completely outside of the tenure track. Because more stable, better paying faculty positions tended to be awarded to men, women often had little choice but to take on low-paying instructorships in composition.

This economic aspect of the feminization of composition teaching was reinforced through the increasing association of composition, especially first-semester and "pre-college" courses, with mechanical correctness. As the Edison advertisement illustrates, popular images associated women with routine, mechanical tasks and men with conceptual tasks: the division between routine work and creative work often defined the gendered division of labor. When typewriters entered the workplace toward the end of the nineteenth century, a century's worth of ideological work had already linked women with what Sharon Hartman Strom calls "light manufacturing" (188). In her history of office work, Strom explains that in the nineteenth century, "the association between women and light manufacturing was already an acceptable image upon which advertisers and employers could draw in establishing the wide-spread use of new machines and the employment of operators in offices" (188). She continues: "The nineteenth century had implanted firm notions of men and women in the industrial world; [white] native-born men were associated with artisanry and craftsmanship, [white] native-born women with light factory work, and immigrants and blacks with manual labor. In the new office, it was desirable to appropriate these notions in familiar but somewhat recast forms" (188).

The logic of associating white women with routine, mechanical work is reproduced in education through the association of white women with mechanical correctness. While "mechanical work" in the corporate office, as in the factory, is literally associated with machines, designating matters of conformity to standardized usage as "mechanical" suggests a figurative association of correctness with work that requires no thought. I will have some things to say about the implications of figuring the ability to work in the conventions of a standardized language as a "mechanical" rather than a mental skill; however, the connection between secretarial work and composition teaching does not hinge upon this transference of the mechanical from the literal to the figurative realm. Mechanical correctness itself functions as an overt link between composition teaching (as it came to be divided from conceptual work) and secretarial work. For example, one writer advised prospective secretaries in 1916 to remember: "It is always possible to write good English, and a secretary must know how; for many business men do not take time to dictate correct English, leaving it to their secretaries to correct errors" (Spencer 51). A writer in 1917 put this injunction a bit more forcefully: "A busy man in dictating letters will often be guilty of errors which would make his letter ridiculous if it were written just as he dictated it" (qtd. in Davies 132). The secretary, like the composition teacher, must take the time to attend to correct English; they must be willing to do the work that men of business and style are too busy to worry about. Because both secretaries and composition teachers have been charged with the duty of attending to mechanical correctness, I will be drawing from sources associated with both occupations in order to get at a better understanding of the cultural values that construct and are constructed by the association of (usually white) women with the "mechanics" of English.

The association of women with the mechanics of language has held and continues to hold a strong place in the public imagination. Gail Stygall notes that, despite the work of feminist linguists to counter this association, women continue to be associated with language conservation rather than with language innovation (261). Just as the image of the woman transcribing her employer's words in the Edison advertisement offers a concrete picture of the gender-coding of mechanical work in the corporate office, so do popular representations of women teachers associate them with routine work generally and mechanical correctness specifically. The association of elementary schoolwork with routine and women with elementary schoolwork coalesces in the figure of the "schoolmarm," the very image of a pathetic, desexualized woman who clings to the enforcement of rules. Charles William Eliot, the president of Harvard who blazed the trail leading to required first-year composition, spoke disparagingly of the "school-dame's practice of giving a copy of nothing but zeros to the child who alleges that he cannot make that figure" (12). Eliot portrayed the practice of teaching through repetitive drill as decidedly a woman's practice, the work of "the school-dame." For at least a century, then, women teachers have been associated with routine work, an association that continued to be played out as women began to teach required writing in colleges. The linking of women with the teaching of grammar is, as Robert Connors has suggested, a "common stereotype" embodied in "[t]he image of a grim-faced Miss Grundy, besprinkling the essays of her luckless students with scarlet handbook hieroglyphs" ("Mechanical" 61). "Miss Grundy" is, like the schoolmarm from whom she descends, a figure not only of routine and grammatical rules but also of a negative version of the feminine—namely, the old maid. What this suggests is not only that routine work—already regarded as less interesting and thus less valuable in the capitalist division of labor—tends to be associated with women but also that women, through their association with routine work, come to be further demeaned. Women teachers are coded as "grim" creatures, reviled for their love of rules as much as for their apparent rejection of sexuality. Mechanical correctness—and, by association, writing instruction—as a result comes to be marginalized yet again: not only is it regarded as nonintellectual, but it is considered the province of joyless spinsters.[6]

That the association of women with the mechanics of writing predates even the influx of women into writing programs is clear in the Harvard committee's 1897 report on student writing. The committee commented with disapproval upon the "extreme crudeness both of thought and execution" in the themes of Harvard men (Adams, Godkin, and Nutter 103). Despite their claim that the themes revealed "crudeness of thought," the committee members tended to focus more upon "execution," pointing out instances of "bad penmanship," "incorrect spelling," "defective punctuation," and "lack of good grammatical expression" (104–5). In turning to themes written by the women students at Radcliffe, however, the committee found a superior handling of mechanics: "In mechanical execution,—neatness, penmanship, punctuation and orthography,—they show a marked superiority in standard over the papers from the courses of the College proper" (108). The committee further praised these papers for showing "a greater degree of conscientious, painstaking effort" (108). Despite these favorable comments, the committee nonetheless was careful to point out that mechanical correctness and painstaking effort was insufficient; the women's themes, the committee maintained, lacked evidence of conceptual work: "In thought and in form, they are less robust and less self-assertive. A few are sprightly; none of them indicate any especial capacity for observing, or attempt, in pointing out defects and difficulties, anything which might be termed a thoughtful solution of them" (108). Even though evidence of conceptual work was also missing from the papers of the male students, and even though the committee commented almost exclusively upon the poor showing of the male students in the area of mechanical execution, the committee effectively labeled the women's writing as inferior to men's writing because of its alleged lack of thought.

An even more striking instance of condemning women for their attention to the mechanics of English occurs in Karl Dykema's 1950 CCCC address, "The Problem of Freshman English in the Liberal Arts College." Dykema, a future chair of the CCCC and professor at Youngstown College, was anxious that composition teachers not devote too much class time to routine matters. Unless freshman English at liberal arts colleges was conducted so as not to "discourage students from electing courses in literature," he worried that "ultimately speech and English departments will be staffed by harmless, dull, unimaginative nonentities" whose "sole qualification is that they are human machines that can spell, punctuate, and capitalize as if they were animated dictionaries and handbooks combined" (4, 5, 3). It becomes clear that Dykema associated these "human machines" with women as he described three hypothetical students. Two students—X and Y—are male; one has trouble with the mechanics of written English, one with spoken English. A third student, Z, is "a girl of mediocre capacity" whose written and spoken English is "mechanically satisfactory," but "she cannot be stimulated to a more accurate, logical, or effective expression of anything because she has nothing to express" (5). According to Dykema, the dilemma he faces is how to grade these three students. He could, he reasons, "set up an arbitrary rule that five misspelled or mispronounced words would automatically mean failure" (5). In this case, X and Y would see that they should fail if they had misspelled or mispronounced five or more words. But how, Dykema wonders, will he be able to convince Z that she too should fail when Z is "too stupid to realize that she has failed to do what was required" (5)? Ultimately, Dykema decides, "it is Z who does not matter, X and Y who do" (6). After all, he sees Z not as a potential student of literature but as someone who "will ultimately vegetate her life away as an excellent typist, preferably for X, who sorely needs her, though strictly in a stenographic capacity" (5). This imaginary woman, in other words, has potential value as a typist—as a "human machine" capable of producing mechanically correct writing—but no value as an intellectual or a future teacher of literature.

This odd academic ambivalence toward mechanical correctness— the coding of it simultaneously as a sign of value and as a sign of lack—points to a similar ambivalence in the corporate world toward secretaries. While it is commonplace to hear employers speak of their secretaries as "the ones who really run things around here," it is also the case that employers tend to define secretaries by what they lack. In her study of representations of secretaries, Rosemary Pringle offers an example of an executive who defines "secretary" as, essentially, "not a boss" (1). Pringle goes on to explain: "If, as the psychoanalysts suggest, 'woman' is perceived as 'lacking' what it takes to be a 'man,' so are secretaries defined as 'lacking' the qualities that make a successful boss. Our executive defines secretaries in negative terms as representing everything that bosses are not" (1).

What secretaries are coded as "lacking" is what the Radcliffe students' themes were said to be lacking—namely, thought. One writer in 1917 advised secretaries to remember that they have time to waste on routine matters; the executive, who must constantly use his brain, does not: "The true executive has not much time for anything but creative work. He can easily waste two or three hours a day by personal attention to his mail" (qtd. in Davies 132). The term "executive," indeed, seems almost a misnomer, given that secretarial workers frequently were described as "those whose daily tasks are the execution of thoughts and orders of business men" (Spencer 5). Businessmen have thoughts; secretaries execute those thoughts. The dichotomy here is exactly the dichotomy evoked by the Harvard committee: the bifurcation of thought, associated with "creative," productive work, from execution of thought, associated with "mechanical," reproductive work.

Given the cultural association of mechanical correctness with nonintellectual work and, thus, with women, the intense scrutiny of college students' writing for signs of error seems curious. How did mechanical correctness come to function as so powerful a sign that the university community and the public at large began to expect that the required course in writing would provide instruction in grammar? Susan Miller has argued that the focus on correctness "allowed written texts to become instruments for examining the 'body' of *a* student, not just *the* student body," so that a teacher may "examine the student's language with the same attitude that controls a medical examination" (57). This symbolic examination of the student's body, according to Miller, suggests that "a pedagogic obsession with mechanical correctness also participated in a broadly conceived nineteenth-century project of cleanliness" (57).

In fact, the association of mechanically well-executed writing with cleanliness and hygiene is apparent throughout twentieth-century descriptions of the importance of "good" writing in the corporate workplace. A 1941 textbook on office management, for example, offers a particularly suggestive analogy: "Just as housewives place more trust in those laundries employing neat drivers and modern delivery equipment, so are businessmen more inclined to establish and continue relations with those concerns whose letters, in form and content, convey an impression of neatness, courtesy, and friendliness" (Neuner and Haynes 46). The importance of "neatness" appears to be equally valuable to laundry service and to business correspondence. The analogy between cleanliness and the mechanics of writing further associates the work with women: one contemporary secretary has commented that "typing is seen as something every woman can do—like washing up!" (qtd. in Pringle 3).

The discourse of hygiene, it must be remembered, functions as more than a discourse of middle-class propriety. To evoke "hygiene" in the late nineteenth and early twentieth centuries was to call forth a chain of linked signifieds, including both personal health and racial health. As late as 1929, books with titles such as *Racial Hygiene: A Practical Discussion of Eugenics and Race Culture* appeared under the imprint of the most reputable New York publishers (T. Rice). To practice good hygiene was to keep the (white) body healthy and the (white) race "pure." This practice was considered to be particularly important for white women, the potential mothers of the future members of the race. The appearance of a person's writing, in the logic of hygienics, was a sign of the appearance of the person: mechanically correct writing was a sign of a correct person—a sign, that is, of a white, native-born American. White women were understood to be "good" women and, because of their purported goodness, would "naturally" be associated with proper, hygienic language use.

While white women were coded as naturally good, women of color were made to "earn" their reputations. Jacqueline Jones Royster points out that as African American women entered institutions of higher education in the late nineteenth and early twentieth centuries, they were expected to *develop* moral character, whereas white women were assumed to *possess* moral character. Royster explains, "For white women, lady-ness . . . was an unmarked category, that is, a natural expectation. For African American women, however, . . . it was a marked category. . . . By stereotype, 'moral' as an identity marker for African American women was acquired, not ascribed" (*Traces* 182). Given the association of "proper" English with "proper" behavior and personhood, it follows that only white women would be associated with mechanical correctness.

If the teaching of composition has been "feminized"—feminized in the sense that composition teaching is regarded as work suitable for women and the mechanics of writing are seen as the special province of women—it has also been racialized. The dissociation of mechanical correctness from intellectual work—a dissociation that emerged with writing programs—lends itself to both tendencies. That is, insofar as the teaching of composition is associated with routine rather than with mental labor, the logic of the capitalist division of labor demands that its workers receive less pay. At the same time, because white women are coded as "naturally" better at routine tasks, it is a simple matter to extend this logic and consider them to be naturally able to produce mechanically correct English. If mechanically correct, standard English is the natural property of white women, it follows that people who are other than white have no claim to this property.[7] Of course, stereotypes are not truth. As Royster's historical study shows, African American women have long been "talented users of language who have demonstrated expertise across multiple measures of performance and achievement" (*Traces* 77). The work of such writers as Anna Julia Cooper and Ida B. Wells provides obvious evidence of the linguistic and rhetorical prowess of African American women (see also Logan, *"We Are Coming"*). Moreover, as Shirley Wilson Logan points out, African American women have a long history of providing literacy education for black students ("'When'" 47–48). Despite this tradition of literacy work, and despite the fact that African American women, like white women, have long found employment as teachers, African American women have rarely been employed to carry out this work among white people (see J. Jones 333; Royster, *Traces* 178).

Writing programs, I have argued, emerged by way of divisions in labor, divisions that separated mental labor, coded as white and masculine, from mechanical labor, coded as white and feminine. Writing programs, thus, function as contradictory sites of (economic) disenfranchisement and (racial) privilege, both drawn along gendered lines. Whether teachers of composition or literature, our work is necessarily entangled with these ideologies that separate meaning from mechanics and that articulate ideologies of gender and race with "proper" uses of language. As teachers of English, we might seek to undo some of these complex articulations. To question the feminization of composition teaching implies more than a questioning of *who* teaches composition. *Who* teaches composition is inextricably linked to *why* composition remains a required course and to *what* the university community expects to be taught in the course. The contingent status of composition teachers is thus more than a labor issue—though it is decidedly that. The economic materiality of the division of labor, which has led to low pay and unstable working conditions, calls for labor struggle. The struggle for better working conditions, however, will not necessarily touch upon the gender and racial codings that required writing—through its association with correctness—continues to carry, despite the work of composition scholars over the last thirty years toward intellectual redefinition of the course. To struggle over these destructive codings requires participation in a larger struggle, one that demands solidarity not simply among all composition teachers and composition professionals but among all whose lives depend upon lasting social change.

## 2

# Teaching Subjects: Professionalism and the Discourse of Disorder

WITH THE TEACHING of first-year writing separated, both materially and ideologically, from the rest of the English department, the blame for the "problem" of college student writing began to shift. Now, not only were high school teachers to blame for the "sorry" state of entering students' writing but so were college composition teachers themselves. Writing in 1940, nine years before the founding of the Conference on College Composition and Communication, in which he would play a leading role, George Wykoff of Purdue University enumerated some of the more prevalent complaints against writing teachers:

> Among the many serious critical charges leveled, from both within and without the profession, against the teaching and teacher of English, the lowly teacher of composition has had more than his just share. Scorned or ignored by those who give courses in literature in graduate and undergraduate schools, he is further bewildered by the mass of specific charges against him: that he stresses grammar which has no relation to writing; that he teaches, as incorrect, expressions which have been in idiomatic good use long enough to be generally accepted; that he emphasizes mechanics when he should be stressing content; that his students, even after years of training, cannot spell, punctuate, or use correct grammar; that his students, even if they do write correctly, have nothing to say. ("Teaching" 426)

Located at the bottom of the hierarchy in English departments, the "lowly teacher of composition" bore the brunt of complaints against English teachers, including ones—like being accused both of stressing grammar *and* of producing writers who cannot use correct grammar—that were at odds. As any contemporary composition specialist can attest, charges like these have by no means gone away. And the response that Wykoff offered—a proposal to professionalize the teaching of writing, treating it as a career for which one receives both training and rewards—continues to reemerge in our contemporary disciplinary discourse. Examining Wykoff's proposal in hindsight, however, we can see not just an iteration of what remains a common theme today but also the seeds from which emerged the field's professional organization, the CCCC. Looking at his analysis, then, gives a glimpse into at least some of the exigencies leading to the founding of the CCCC.

Wykoff, who directed "English I" (first-year composition) at Purdue for over thirty years, attempted to take the blame off the composition teacher and to identify external causes for the allegedly sorry state of composition teaching:

> Though shouldering the blame, the English teacher refuses to believe that the fundamental difficulty—largely through no fault of his own—lies in himself. He never dares speak out boldly to the graduate schools that gave him no training for teaching composition; to his administrative superiors who give him no incentive for even trying to do good work; and to both for stifling whatever interest he may once, in his salad days, have had for the task. Yet, if you want to find out why English teachers are not successfully teaching composition, look at their training, their incentives, and their lack of interest. In other words, if a teacher consciously chooses composition as a career, what can be his training, making use of present-day facilities, and what can be his rewards (since man can live neither by bread—nor by themes—alone)? ("Teaching" 428)

It seems clear that Wykoff identified some problems attending the *labor* of composition teaching to be nonetheless the responsibility of management. While labor—the composition teachers themselves—may have been the problem, they couldn't be blamed for that. While Wykoff did not deny that many teachers might have been doing a

subpar job, he believed the administrators of the course (both directors who might have offered training and departmental and college
administrators who might have offered incentives) ought to at least
have shared responsibility. The administrators hadn't provided training in graduate school for teaching composition, and they failed to
provide any kind of incentive or development for the job. One of
these alleged failures—the need for incentives—speaks to the need
to properly compensate teachers. Wykoff, however, gives much more
attention in his article to the question of training, which takes up
two pages of his text, than to incentives, which takes up less than
one. Wykoff did envision a "Utopia" in which teachers have better working conditions—"The teaching-load is nine hours a week:
two sections of elementary composition (each limited to twenty
students), one of advanced composition (limited to fifteen students)"
(433)—but also more time for professional development, "to belong
to, read the publications of, and take part in the affairs of, certain
national and state organizations" (436) (and time to participate in
a number of other activities, including keeping up with research,
having conferences each week with students, and communicating
closely with high school teachers). Even these imagined conditions,
in other words, point more toward the need for professional development than for better working conditions and compensation.

Wykoff continued this line of thought in a 1948 address at the
National Council of Teachers of English (NCTE) conference, is-
suing a "clarion call" for greater scholarly attention to first-year
composition that led, in the following year, to the first meeting of
the CCCC in Chicago in 1949 ("Chicago Convention," 286). In that
NCTE address, which some see as the very inspiration for the formation of this new organization, Wykoff continued to call for greater
professional development but made quite a significant distinction
between "ourselves, that is, those who . . . do have an interest in
freshman composition and who would like to make progress toward
what a good composition teacher should be" and "our colleagues in
composition" ("Toward" 319, 320). The latter group included "graduate assistants hoping that the Ph.D. will help them to escape, . . .
young Ph.D.'s who are reading themes while they make a reputation

in literary scholarship, . . . literature specialists who occasionally draw a section or two of composition" (321). "Whoever they are and however long they have freshman composition to teach," Wykoff asserted, "they should be persuaded to realize that this course is worth as much time, effort, and energy as any course in literature" (321).

It has been claimed that the CCCC was founded to meet the needs of teachers of composition (see, for instance, Crowley, "Early"), and understanding the CCCC as a teacher-oriented organization fits with composition studies' understanding of itself as what Joseph Harris has called a "teaching subject." However, as Wykoff's distinction makes clear, there are teachers of composition, and then there are colleagues who teach composition. The CCCC was founded by the former, in part to better "persuade" the latter to bring more devotion to their job. Insofar as the CCCC was established for the benefit of composition teachers, then, composition teachers were conceived to be those who *cared* about the teaching of composition, who had a positive affective relationship to the course; it was also founded as a way of changing the attitude of those who did not care, who had a more neutral or even negative affective relationship toward the subject. Composition teachers' needs, then, were perceived more often to be needs for better training and greater coordination rather than for the better pay or greater job security that a feminized position seems almost by definition to call for. In other words, teachers' needs were seen more from the point of view of management, from those who already cared about the teaching of composition—focusing on what could rather more easily be provided, in the form of training—than consistently from the point of view of those delivering the course and providing surplus labor for the English department. Indeed, Wykoff never mentioned actually talking to the "colleagues" in composition but instead constructed an administrator's list of what would benefit them.

Through a close reading of additional documents from others among the CCCC's founders, this chapter will demonstrate that these men and women, like Wykoff himself, while well-intentioned, ultimately focused more on meeting the needs of composition "professionals"—directors of freshman composition and the then-popular communication course and others who already aligned themselves with composition—than on addressing the material needs of teachers, including those who felt less aligned with the composition course. Indeed, drawing on the trope that Wykoff both repeated and critiqued, the early CCCC discourse frequently and repeatedly figured teachers as the problem of the composition course, as disorganized masses in need of systematic intervention. In making professional-managers' concerns a priority, the processes of class hierarchy and the gendering of writing programs described in the previous chapter were further reinforced. The CCCC, to put it another way, became a site for the propagation of discourse to create proper *teaching subjects*.

I am putting a decided twist here on Harris's claim that the field of composition studies is primarily a "teaching subject," "that part of English studies which defines itself through an interest in the work students and teachers do together" (*Teaching* ix). In his book *A Teaching Subject*, Harris shifts the focus of composition studies away from what he sees as an increasing professional interest in the production of knowledge about writing and toward what he considers to be composition studies' true domain—the *practices* of teaching writing. The field of composition studies, according to this view, is a *teaching* subject because it takes the teaching of writing as its central concern.

But during the same time that Harris was writing his history of the field, in the late 1980s and early 1990s, a thoroughgoing investigation of the very idea of a "subject" was well under way. Poststructuralist theory emerged almost simultaneously with the post–open admissions growth of composition studies as a field of study (a phenomenon I'll address in more detail in chapter 3). A "subject," for a poststructuralist writer like Michel Foucault, is more than a field of knowledge: it is the person who comes into being as a result of subjection to that knowledge. For Susan Miller, for instance, the field of composition studies is a power/knowledge complex for the construction of *student subjects*, a position that I supported in the previous chapter: required writing was certainly a means of managing the growing student body in postbellum colleges and universities. In addition to constructing student subjects through pedagogical means, however, composition studies also operates to construct *teaching subjects.* In other words, composition studies is more than simply a subject about teaching and more than a body of knowledge that seeks to produce proper student subjects; it is a power/knowledge complex devoted, in the words of the founding members of the CCCC, to the "development of teachers who possess and can demonstrate a clear and professional superiority in the arts of language" ("Administration" 41).

Although the analysis of power/knowledge has long been misunderstood as an analysis of systems of oppression, Foucault's project was to make visible that which makes possible (the French *pouvoir* is both a noun, "power," and a verb, "to enable"), that which leads to the emergence of the new. The power/knowledge complex produced through CCCC discourse, then, is not necessarily coercive. All the same, it is crucial to see that the development of proper teaching subjects through the systematic circulation of power/knowledge has been a defining characteristic of the movement to professionalize composition teaching, which is the movement that led to the CCCC. Far from being a very recent phenomenon that threatens to remove composition studies from its focus on teaching practices, professionalization is what has made composition studies—as a set of pedagogical practices and a body of knowledge about those practices—possible. The previous chapter's description of the emergence of hierarchical writing programs, along with Wykoff's observations excerpted above on the burdens shouldered by the teachers, demonstrate that the teachers of composition have been at the bottom of the hierarchy, economically and culturally. This chapter takes up the emergence of the person just above the teachers in that hierarchy, the person charged with directing what was then often called simply "freshman English," and that person's relation to the teachers whose work he (or, more rarely, she) was supervising. The founding of the CCCC, I will argue, marks the most overt emergence of that figure, a person who, by way of his or her position, is involved in a class process of overseeing the production and distribution of the teachers' surplus labor.

Even as I endorse an understanding of professional/managerial control as not necessarily coercive, as discussed in this book's introduction, I nonetheless will demonstrate how professionalism in composition studies has tended to enfranchise those involved in the administration of composition more than it has enfranchised the vast majority of teachers of composition. Scholarship in the field has attempted to discipline teachers, to provide a way of teaching, rather than address the material conditions of teaching. I will show that the early participants in the CCCC tended to identify the problem of composition teaching much more with misinformed teachers than with the materiality of the division of labor. The solution to the so-called problem of the undisciplined teacher was conceived of as professional discipline: more systematic management, better training, and better knowledge. The reward of this discipline for teachers was rarely improvement in the conditions of their work but ideally a better product for the consumers (that is, students).

## PROFESSIONALISM, MANAGERIALISM, AND THE QUESTION OF CONTROL

Over the course of the first half of the twentieth century, directors of first-year composition were most often drawn from the ranks of tenured faculty in the English department and so were most often specialists in a literary field or in linguistics. With very few exceptions (Michigan's rhetoric program under Fred Newton Scott, for instance), advanced degrees in rhetoric or composition were unavailable until the 1970s. Those who directed first-year composition, then, like those who taught it, rarely had any special expertise in the area. George Wykoff, for instance, chair of English I at Purdue for over thirty years, studied eighteenth-century literature as a master's student at Columbia and later as a postgraduate student at the University of Chicago, although he apparently never completed the PhD (see Rose 230–33). His publications and work in composition teaching, however, far outnumbered his accomplishments in eighteenth-century literature. According to Shirley K. Rose, a later successor of Wykoff's at Purdue, he supervised "both junior and senior professorial faculty—more junior than senior—and a few part-time lecturers in the English department" (223). The labor situation, then, though different, was nonetheless fraught. Rather than a majority of part-time lecturers, this "average" department (as described in a 1949 *College English* report, "Chicago Convention" 286) employed a large number of tenure-track instructors (the rank in which Wykoff was originally hired). In order to achieve tenure and to move into the professorial ranks, these instructors had to publish in their areas of expertise. At the same time, they were teaching primarily heavy loads of composition. It is no wonder, given that what was rewarded was research and that there was not yet a research field for composition scholarship, that most teachers of composition would see it as something to be overcome rather than to be devoted to. Wykoff and others like him, however, sought to professionalize these teachers, to shift their devotion from scholarship in literary studies to the teaching and researching of composition.

Before analyzing the discourse of professionalism in the early years of the CCCC, I want to clarify how I am using the term. In his critique of the discourse of professionalism in rhetorical studies, Robert Hariman describes a profession as "a community of skilled workers characterized by a distinct body of knowledge, a code of ethics, and peer review" (214). Professionalism emerged as a dominant discourse for compartmentalizing work and privatizing knowledge in the late nineteenth century, giving rise to a new middle class. It allowed this new class to "continue their assault upon those privileges withheld by the aristocrats above them while protecting their newly won gains from the immigrant hordes pouring in below" (215). The discourse of professionalism, further, made possible the new university: whereas the antebellum American college was chiefly a place for the cultivation of the "learned" professions of medicine, law, and the ministry, the university in the late nineteenth century became a place that provided certification for an ever-growing number of middle-class professions, including pharmacy, business, and school teaching (see Bledstein for a more detailed accounting of the rise of these professions).

Hariman thus argues that professionalism forms the central ethos of university culture and, further, that "understanding American intellectual discourse requires a critique of professionalism . . . as the dominant apparatus of power shaping our rules for determining truthfulness and probity" (212). Drawing from Foucault's analysis of power/knowledge, Hariman develops a set of claims concerning the role of professionalism in the production of knowledge. The first of these claims is that "knowledge is a product of a specific system of social control" (216). In particular, academic knowledge, organized into discrete disciplines, is a product of what Foucault refers to as "discipline." Hariman argues that "expertise is the fundamental instrument in the disciplinary system. Disciplinary power is the exercise of the authority coming from expertise" (216–17). Expertise is "disciplined behavior, behavior marked by strict conformity to procedure" (217). One of the central claims I will develop about the CCCC, extending from this analysis of professional expertise, is that it was founded in order to produce disciplinary knowledge that would make possible disciplined teaching subjects.

Hariman's second claim draws from Foucault's description of the panopticon to argue that "disciplinary knowledge is produced by a process of spatialization" (218). Hariman explains:

> The establishment of a discipline proceeds by identifying a separate space for inquiry and proceeds best if the investigation is identified with a separate administrative domain in the society, as psychiatry was joined with the asylum, and education with the school. . . . In every case the knower becomes an administrator—directed to observe in order to maintain the normal condition of the space. (219)

This point—that professional knowledge is spatialized knowledge and, further, that this separate space requires an administrative eye in order to maintain a separate domain—is crucial in understanding the CCCC and the development of composition studies. I will argue that the knowledge produced with the founding of the CCCC is knowledge that is geared toward the management of teachers and that the spatialized knowledge about the teaching of composition serves primarily to maintain the "separate administrative domain" of composition teaching.

The necessity of spatialization in order to produce disciplinary knowledge is one reason the study and administration of composition teaching has emerged only recently as a profession. As I demonstrated in the previous chapter, writing programs came to be seen as separate from the rest of the English department only in the two decades before World War II. Thus, the administrator of composition would have seen himself or herself as producing knowledge that could be subsumed under the larger category of "English." The process of spatialization that made possible the field of composition studies can be mapped through a series of increasingly specialized journals. Although it now focuses primarily upon secondary school English, the *English Journal*, founded in 1912 as the official organ of the National Council of Teachers of English, for many years also published articles on the teaching of English in colleges and universities. In the late 1920s, around the same time that debates about the proper administration of freshman English began to emerge, the *English Journal* began to publish a separate college edition. *College English*, devoted, as the name suggests, to English at the postsecondary level, began publication in 1939; one of the articles published during its first year was George Wykoff's "Teaching Composition as a Career." Eleven years later, *College Composition and Communication* premiered as the official organ of the newly organized Conference on College Composition and Communication, signaling the emergence of an enclosed space for the study of the first-year course in English composition and communication.

A second reason for the late emergence of composition as a professional discourse, I would argue, is linked to the contradiction between the university as a place of "freedom" and individuality and the composition course as a site for required, enforced behaviors (see Strickland, "How to Compose a Capitalist"). Although, as I have shown in chapter 1, writing programs functioned according to managerial logic long before the CCCC was founded, it was only with the emergence of the New Deal and Keynesian economics after World War II that managed state intervention was extended into what had formerly been considered private domains. With the more thorough saturation of everyday life with managerial logic, the required composition course and the supervised teaching staff were no longer at odds with the dominant cultural logic.

Managerial logic, in other words, fundamentally proceeds out of professional culture. Once organizations of any kind are organized hierarchically, with a class of experts structuring and overseeing the work of a group of nonexperts, management happens. Professionalism calls for control and systematization of knowledge, and management is that group of people who enforce that.

This extension from professionalism into managerialism can be seen in the history of public school teaching. Indeed, Jurgen Herbst has called the professionalization of public education "the betrayal of the teacher" because of the way that advancement in schools came to be equated with a movement out of the classroom. Herbst writes:

> Judged by the sociologists' criteria—professional or graduate training comparable to that of lawyers or physicians; professional autonomy in the workplace; professional guidance through a code of ethics; performance evaluation by peers; immediate responsibility toward clients and ultimate accountability to society—administrators and specialists, not the teachers, are seen as the professionals in public education. Professionalization thus is held out to teachers if they are willing to leave the classroom. (8)

For Herbst, it isn't professionalization itself that is the problem but the way in which professional autonomy and advancement is offered primarily to administrators rather than to teachers. Moreover, Herbst points out that, not unlike the division I traced in chapter 1, the division in public schools tends to be gendered, with more women in the classroom and more men in administrative roles.

As I explained in the introduction, drawing from Raymond Williams, "administration," the preferred term for supervision in education and other public sector institutions, is simply a "polite" term for management. Although a management guru and thus a not unbiased source, Peter Drucker nonetheless offers the idea that management, much like rhetoric, is a generic function:

> Management, that is, the organ of leadership, directions, and decision in our social institutions, and especially in business enterprise, is a *generic function* which faces the same basic tasks

in every country and, essentially, in every society. Management has to give direction to the institution it manages. It has to think through the institution's mission, has to set its objectives, and has to organize resources for the results the institution has to contribute. (17)

In fact, Antonio Gramsci offers what we might call a very similar theory of management within his theory of hegemony. As I have pointed out elsewhere, borrowing from Gramsci's translators, the verb *dirigere* occurs frequently in Gramsci's *Prison Notebooks* to refer to two distinct concepts: on the one hand, "power based on domination," and on the other, "the exercise of 'direction' or 'hegemony'" (Hoare and Smith xiii; see also my "The Managerial Unconscious"). *Dirigere* also in common usage means "to manage." To direct or manage a group of people, then, can suggest either that one dominates them or that one provides guidance, a leading into new possibility. Intellectuals, according to Gramsci, provide direction; their role is *dirigere*. The question is what sort of direction and thus what sort of intellectual one will be.

Traditional intellectuals, according to Gramsci, are indeed functionaries: "The intellectuals are the dominant group's 'deputies' exercising the subaltern functions of social hegemony and political government" (Gramsci 12). Professional discourse, following this formulation, is a discourse that exercises this deputy function, exercising limits on what can and cannot be done within a given profession. Managers are the people who embody this function. However, Gramsci also indicates that hegemony isn't static, that there is always what he understands to be a struggle for hegemony, for leadership. As part of this process, traditional intellectuals are assimilated, becoming not organic intellectuals (that is, leaders in the struggle for a new hegemonic formation) but rather allies. Moreover, these intellectuals can "direct" the work of their peers—fellow holders of traditional professional credentials—by providing what Chantal Mouffe refers to as vocabulary for the struggle.

For some more recent theorists, however, Gramsci's theory of hegemony is insufficient for explaining how people actually are moved to act in that it offers too much of a "rational" account, depending upon conscious beliefs and commitments. Jon Beasley-Murray, in the preface to his book *Posthegemony*, describes the Spanish *Requirimento*, a text that the Conquistadors were required to read to Native populations in the Americas before attacking them (it offered the Natives the opportunity to freely consent before being forced to submit to Christendom and Spain). While, according to Gramsci's theory of hegemony, the *Requirimento* would seem to be a perfect hegemonic text, one offering the opportunity for free consent prior to forced subjugation, Beasley-Murray argues that insofar as it communicated nothing to the Native populations (being both in Spanish, which they did not understand, and in legal discourse, which likely even the Conquistadors did not understand), it was not an ideological document. It did not shape the conscious beliefs of anyone. Rather, it functioned at the level of affect and habit, its repetition functioning as a ritual by which the Conquistadors' "desires were synchronized and unified as part of a joint project" (3).

The *Requirimento*, then, functioned as a managerial text, shaping not so much the rational decisions of those who were spoken to but rather the attitudes and thus the actions of those who spoke. Managerial discourse in general shapes desires and seeks to create the felt sense of a shared project. It too may habituate intellectuals to the role of functionary, supporting the status quo. And it is in this way, I want to argue, that the early discourse of the CCCC worked. It created the sense of a shared project, which is not in itself a bad thing. But like the Spanish *Requirimento* and most professional-managerial discourses, it all too often shapes the desires of those involved in their production and repetition without consideration of the material effects on those being managed. I do not mean to suggest, of course, that managerial discourse is necessarily equivalent to Empire, a claim that would be surely hyperbolic.[1] Nonetheless, there is certainly in managerial discourse a tendency to discount the lived needs of those being managed in favor of the felt sense of rightness.

The discourse of the early CCCC, while indicating some concern for situations and for the material conditions of teaching first-year writing, nonetheless indicates more of an impulse to fix standards, to normalize by establishing what is and is not a proper first-year writing course. This professionalizing impulse, as Hariman points out, is very much the working-out of a class process, establishing the territory of the "middle class" as between capital and labor. As I will demonstrate in the following section, a discourse that located problems with the teaching of first-year writing *within* teachers set the stage for a discourse that would create further boundaries between the expert composition professional and the inexpert teaching masses, not by creating a set of beliefs, necessarily, but by habituating members of the CCCC to the feeling that they shared a joint project, one from which the masses were affectively separated.

### THE CCCC AND THE POLITICS OF INTERVENTION

The alleged problems with the teaching of first-year writing thus led to a professionalizing impetus that coalesced in 1949 with the formation of the CCCC and, in the following year, with the publication of the organization's flagship journal, *College Composition and Communication* (*CCC*). However, as I've been suggesting, the role of the composition professional slid quite quickly from teacher to administrator: to devote one's career to composition, if the career was to have the security of tenure, meant devoting oneself to the management and normalizing of composition teaching. The director of freshman English was the intermediary between the English department faculty and the largely non-tenure-track composition faculty, setting the conditions for controlled productivity that would benefit the student-consumer.

The CCCC at its founding was dedicated exclusively to the required first-year course in composition (or to the then-popular course in "communication," which combined writing and speaking), especially to questions of how best to conduct the class.[2] The organization began the publication of *CCC* less than a year after its founding. Given its close emergence with the organization itself, *CCC* provides a wealth of information about the concerns of the founding members of this organization. Most of the articles published during the 1950s, for example, were first delivered as papers at the spring meetings, and the journal also printed reports from each of the conference workshops. Despite the availability of this material, however, little has been written about the early history of the CCCC.

In fact, in maintaining that the founding of the CCCC marks the emergence of the composition professional, I am departing from some of the more familiar arguments from earlier histories of composition. Stephen North, for example, rejects the founding of the CCCC as a starting point for his story of the development of what he calls Composition with a capital *C*; he argues instead that the moment of origin for Composition was the publication of research on writing in the 1960s (9).[3] All the same, it does seem strange that composition studies, a field that has been so invested in stories of origin—whether the point of origin is located in ancient Greece, in nineteenth-century America, or in the very recent past—should seem somewhat indifferent toward telling the story of its own professional organization, the CCCC. While the history of the required composition course and the pedagogical and rhetorical theories of those early courses have been repeatedly revisited (in, for example, Connors, *Composition-Rhetoric*; Berlin, *Rhetoric and Reality* and *Writing Instruction*; and Crowley, *Composition*), a history of the CCCC that does more than chronicle its development has, as Kathryn Flannery observed over ten years ago, "yet to be written" (218). James Berlin, for example, devotes a few pages to the development of the CCCC in *Rhetoric and Reality*; however, he is interested less in the significance of the CCCC as a professional organization and more in the setting it provides for competing pedagogical theories. As a result, he represents the early CCCC as a site for struggle between the then-popular "communications" course, which, he maintains, emphasized "the social basis of rhetoric and its importance in a democratic society," and the traditional composition course, which he represents as being mired in the so-called current-traditionalist mode of rhetoric (107).

Late in the last century, as calls to address the problem of contingent labor in composition teaching became ever stronger, Sharon Crowley attempted to recover the history of the CCCC by articulating it with more recent efforts to improve the working conditions of non-tenure-track composition teachers. She maintains that the CCCC "was founded, not to advance knowledge, . . . but in order to help its teachers manage the universally required course and to protect them from exploitation" ("Composition's Ethic" 230). This set of concerns led Crowley, in a 1998 CCCC presentation, to call for the leaders and members of this organization to return to the "spirit of the early CCCC" and to commit themselves "to improving the working conditions of teachers of the first-year course" ("Early"). However, to "help" and "protect" can all too easily slip into a kind of paternalism, and the early CCCC indeed tended toward control, based on expert knowledge, more than toward the reform of exploitative working conditions.

The line between economic help and paternalistic control is, without a doubt, a tenuous one. Roosevelt's New Deal, which preceded the founding of the CCCC by sixteen years, had heralded the emergence of the interventionist state—the extension of systems of management into the political and economic spheres. Ernesto Laclau and Chantal Mouffe refer to the Keynesian Welfare State as "an ambiguous and complex phenomenon" that has served simultaneously to subordinate the labor force to the needs of capital and to bring "real and important benefits to the workers" (161, 162). The founding of the CCCC, a professional organization that set itself up to intervene in the lives of composition teachers through the systematization of information about teaching, represents a similarly ambiguous and complex phenomenon. The CCCC was founded as a forum for the systematization of the composition course—a concern that reflects the importance of management and the subordination of teachers. As already mentioned, directors of composition were not necessarily teachers of composition (indeed, they had most often been trained as literary scholars); rather, their function was to coordinate and oversee those who were teaching the course. All too often in composition scholarship, the field of composition studies and the work of the CCCC has stood in for "composition teaching." While both composition teachers and composition administrators participate actively in the CCCC, it is important to maintain a distinction between the concerns of these two groups because efforts to professionalize groups of workers have historically functioned instead to create a managerial class and, simultaneously, to disenfranchise the very group that such efforts set out to assist by subordinating workers to the needs of capital.[4] Given the CCCC's recent interest in labor issues—an interest that is, without a doubt, well-intentioned—it is crucial that we disentangle the discourse of professionalism from the discourse of labor activism. In order to do this work of disentanglement, we need to return to the moment when a distinct discourse of professionalism began to emerge.

The literature that appeared after the founding of the CCCC is characterized by an increasingly negative view of teachers as chaotic, disordered bodies in need of professional discipline. The discourse of professional intervention, in other words, identified the problem of teaching labor as a behavioral one: rather than locating the problem in the hierarchical division of labor, the discourse of professionalism that emanated from the CCCC tended to locate the problem with the teachers: they didn't know enough; they weren't properly supervised; they weren't properly devoted to their work; they were confused. The founding members of the CCCC set as their goal the development of a systematic body of knowledge that would discipline the teacher. In short, just as the Keynesian state did not overthrow a divisive economic system but rather sought to sustain that system by intervening in the lives of workers, so did (and does) the professional discourse of the CCCC retain a hierarchical division of labor while developing a body of knowledge that would produce docile teaching subjects. While the discourse of professionalism has produced an impressive body of knowledge about writing and the teaching of writing, it has also tended to subordinate the needs of teachers to the needs of writing programs (which represent themselves as subordinate to the needs of the university as a whole and to the consumer-student) and has elevated consumerism—that is, the consumption of pedagogical theory—as the duty of all composition teachers.[5]

### PATHOLOGIZING THE TEACHER

By 1949, the year that the CCCC was founded, the divisions of labor that characterize contemporary writing programs—as described in chapter 1—were ubiquitous and formed a particular area of concern for the early conference participants. The problem of labor, however, as the excerpts from George Wykoff's article at the opening of this chapter suggests, was only secondarily presented, if at all, as an economic problem. Instead, the problem was located in the kind of people being employed to teach composition. In fact, as I will show, the confusion and neurosis of the teacher has continued to be the "problem" that much composition scholarship sets out to cure.

Two early statements defining the challenges facing the person in charge of freshman writing classes were made at the 1950 CCCC convention. Adolphus J. Bryan of Louisiana State University, in "The Problem of Freshman English in the University," and Karl Dykema of Youngstown College, in "The Problem of Freshman English in the Liberal Arts College," identified the quality of the teaching staff as central concerns. For his part, Bryan maintained that "the difficulty of maintaining an adequate and competent staff" is "the Freshman English problem peculiar to universities" (6). He attributed the problem of staffing to two tendencies: first, the tendency for young PhDs to try to "escape from composition teaching . . . through promotion" by publishing scholarly articles, and second, "the use of graduate students in large numbers to take over the teaching of classes in Freshman English" (6). His proposed solution to the first tendency was to effectively separate the teaching of composition from research: "I certainly would lend encouragement to research; but as a Chairman of Freshman English, I should say that there are perhaps on every staff men who ought to be forbidden the opportunity, for they produce at the neglect of their freshman teaching" (7). Bryan, in other words, proposed to actively intervene in the lives of composition instructors and to forbid them from publishing research. It must be remembered that Bryan was an advocate for composition teaching; he wanted to ensure better teaching by maintaining a staff devoted to composition. His suggestion that composition teachers be prevented from pursuing research problems was not the suggestion of someone who was trying to marginalize composition: rather, he hoped to establish a staff devoted to the teaching of composition by setting limits on their professional activities.

While Bryan suggested that young PhDs might be discouraged from doing research in order to more effectively fit them for composition teaching, he realized that the practice of employing graduate students to teach composition presented a more formidable challenge. He noted that even the most conscientious graduate assistant finds "the temptation to neglect his teaching for his graduate work too strong to resist" (7). Bryan, however, offered no solution for this problem; he knew that the economic justification for the use of graduate students was too great:

> Freshman English becomes one of the main supports for the advanced undergraduate and graduate program in a university, first, because in most institutions the hiring of teaching fellows for a freshman course reduces the per capita cost of instruction in the whole department to a figure that won't frighten the dean, and secondly, because the creating of jobs for prospective graduate students furnishes easy justification for the stipends with which we lure these students to graduate school. (7)

Given the economic logic supporting the staffing of freshman English, Bryan finally resolved that he had no solution but would welcome discussion of this issue. Nonetheless, it is clear that Bryan considered it essential to find some way of exerting limits on teachers of composition as a way of keeping them devoted to their work. He wanted, in other words, to somehow shape the behavior of composition teachers, to encourage them to subject themselves to permanent division from the rest of the English department and thereby to become proper teaching subjects.

While divisions of labor created particular kinds of problems for universities, the question of labor—specifically, of the proper sort of person suited to the teaching of English—was no less an issue for Dykema, a professor at a liberal arts college. Whereas Bryan was concerned that composition teachers might devote too much time to research and lose interest in teaching composition, Dykema, as I mentioned in the previous chapter, was worried that teachers tended to give too much time to routine matters and so caused students to lose interest. Dykema conceded that teaching mechanics is an important part of the freshman course, but he sought "to prevent the necessary insistence on mechanical competence from destroying the student's potential interest in writing and literature" (4).

Dykema clearly connected the teaching of mechanics with a certain kind of subject—namely, with women. As I have shown in chapter 1, Dykema described a female student's work as mechanically correct but uninteresting because "she has nothing to express" (5). Dykema worried that if creative young men were deterred from taking courses in literature because they found their freshman English class too tedious, then "our speech and English majors are going to include too many Z's"—"those dull creatures whose sole qualification is that they are human machines that can spell, punctuate, and capitalize as if they were animated dictionaries and handbooks combined" (5, 3). Dykema wanted to rid English departments of these "human machines"—or, at least, exert more control over their behavior—so that they would not continue to reproduce themselves. He wanted teaching subjects who could stimulate thought so that literature classes would be frequented by intelligent men rather than by dull women. In other words, Dykema wanted certain kinds of teachers of freshman English because he wanted certain kinds of consumers of literature classes.

Both Bryan and Dykema indicated that the kind of person teaching freshman English was a central concern among the founding members of the CCCC because they wanted to encourage certain types of behavior and discourage others. On the one hand, Bryan was concerned that teachers of freshman English at universities might devote too much attention to research and neglect the teaching of composition. On the other hand, Dykema worried that English departments might become overrun with "human machines"— feminized subjects who supposedly lacked thought but who could spell and punctuate. Here we have a central dilemma in composition studies: How do we ensure that teachers devote time to more than the mechanics of writing while, at the same time, remaining committed to teaching composition more than to doing research? Moreover, how do we develop a staff that is, in Bryan's words, "competent" and, in Dykema's formulation, not composed of dull, unimaginative "machines"? By focusing upon the quality and behavior of the persons teaching composition rather than upon the material circumstances in which they were teaching (while still acknowledging that those circumstances were not the best), the founding members of the CCCC were participating in and contributing to a discourse that identified labor problems within the worker rather than within the labor process and sought solutions in administrative decisions that involved shaping the behavior of teachers rather than in any sort of larger systemic change. In so doing, they were enacting a class process, one that further exacerbated the class division between composition teachers and composition administrators: the former produced teaching, the latter directed that production.

Bryan and Dykema were by no means the only voices locating the problem of composition teaching within the teacher. Participants in a 1950 workshop on the administration of the composition course suggested that "the problem of staff training is perhaps the most crucial concern" for administrators ("Administration" 40). They accurately noted that "few teachers have had specific training for the job of teaching writing" and argued that obtaining such training was the teacher's "duty" to the profession: "Raising the standards of the profession is to some extent a collective enterprise. It can be done by establishing the legitimacy of our subject matter, and we can demonstrate the importance of our subject matter only by studying it. If composition teachers are to gain the prestige which they seek they must earn and deserve it" (40). Knowledge about the teaching of composition was elevated as a heal-all: "Most of the problems in the teaching of composition [depend] upon the development of teachers who can demonstrate a clear and professional superiority in the arts of language" (41). The problem with this logic is that it blames the teacher for the economic status of composition teaching and suggests that it is up to the teacher to gain knowledge, rather than to work for economic reform, in order to improve that status.

In fact, conference participants could be quite blunt in blaming the teacher. Members of a 1951 workshop on the professional status of the composition teacher, composed primarily of former and current chairs of freshman English courses and English departments, determined that if composition teachers suffered from low status, those teachers were at least partially to blame for this condition.[6] Because they taught composition the same way year after year and experimented so little, "teachers of composition may themselves be partly responsible for the low esteem in which they feel that they are held, and for the 'stigma' attached to their work" ("Professional" 10). This complaint echoes Dykema's charge against teachers who are "dull" and goes quite far in laying the blame at the feet of the teacher.

The problem teacher is a trope that continues through some of the classic texts in composition studies published from the 1960s through the 1980s.[7] In *The Composing Processes of Twelfth Graders*, for instance, Janet Emig depicts secondary school teachers of writing as pathologically confused and pathologically obsessed with mechanical correctness (an obsession that is, I have argued, gender-coded):

> Much of the teaching of writing in American high schools is essentially a neurotic activity. There is little evidence, for example, that the persistent pointing out of specific errors in student themes leads to the elimination of these errors, yet teachers expend much of their energy in this futile and unrewarding exercise. . . . Even the student who, because of the health of his private life, stays somewhat whole is enervated by worries over peripherals—spelling, punctuation, length. (94)

According to this depiction of the teacher and the student, which in many ways evokes Dykema's picture of the human machine who tires out otherwise creative students with her attention to mechanical details, the teacher is clearly the problem.[8] The student, whom Emig describes as having a healthy private life, suffers from the pathology of the teacher.

Of course, Emig's criticism was directed at secondary school teachers; the criticism of secondary school teachers has a history at least as old as the composition course itself, as I've already suggested. Nonetheless, Emig's study is certainly part of the "canon" of composition scholarship, and figuring the teacher as problem has been a trope of composition scholarship. Peter Elbow, after all, advocates writing *without* teachers. Ira Shor, also deploying organic metaphors, calls for the "withering away" of the teacher. Such agendas as Elbow's and Shor's have been praised as "student-centered," although, more recently, they have been criticized for their tendency to disempower teachers, particularly women teachers (see Luke and Gore).

The teacher-as-problem trope appears, moreover, in scholarship that does not explicitly call for the disappearance of the teacher. Richard Fulkerson, for example, in his "Four Philosophies of Composition," explains that he is offering a taxonomy of approaches to the teaching of writing in order to overcome teachers' "consistent mindlessness about relating means to desired ends" (3). In a similar vein, Berlin presents his own taxonomy in response to his conviction that "[t]he dismay students display about writing is . . . at least occasionally the result of teachers unconsciously offering contradictory advice about composing—guidance grounded in assumptions that simply do not square with each other" ("Contemporary Composition" 10). He refers to the "nagging (albeit legitimate) query of the overworked writing teacher: But what does all this have to do with the teaching of freshman composition?" (20).

Teachers in these texts are represented as "mindless" and "nagging," as doing things without thinking about them (much like Dykema's human machine). They seem to be a dysfunctional set of people in need of training. These representations of teachers need not be true (or false, for that matter) to keep in circulation the *felt need* for professional intervention. The most important function of these representations of teachers as disordered masses, thus, was to reinforce the sense that experts in the administration of composition courses were necessary. In the next section, I will demonstrate that the CCCC set itself up to provide the administrative space and professional knowledge for disciplining teachers into proper behaviors.

### THE CURE: SYSTEM AND KNOWLEDGE

Both Bryan and Dykema, in their separate meditations on the problems of freshman English, reveal anxiety over how best to control the teaching of composition. In fact, expressions of the need to systematize and exert control over the teaching of this course characterize the early CCCC. This need was expressed as the desire to develop a body of knowledge about the teaching of composition and to normalize—through the deployment of effective management—the teaching of composition at the local level.

Although Crowley has claimed that the CCCC was not founded in order to advance knowledge, the evidence of early statements published in *CCC* clearly suggests that developing a research agenda was, in fact, a primary concern of this organization's founding members. John Gerber, the first chairman of the CCCC, reported in the premier issue of *CCC* that the organization was formed precisely because teachers of the first-year course "have had no systematic way of exchanging views and information quickly" nor "means of developing a coordinated research program" (12). He further expressed hope that through this exchange of information, "the standards of the profession will be raised" (12). Moreover, the original constitution of the CCCC, published in 1952, lists three primary objectives, each of which relates to administration or to knowledge-building: "The specific objects are: (1) to provide an opportunity for discussions of problems relating to the organization and teaching of college composition and communications courses, (2) to encourage studies and research in the field, and (3) to publish a bulletin containing reports of conferences and articles of interest to teachers of composition and communication" ("Constitution" 19).

In addition to building knowledge, the early participants in the CCCC were particularly concerned with systematizing the first-year course, as is evident in the list of workshop topics from the 1950 conference: "The Function of the Composition Course in General Education," "Objectives and Organization of the Composition Course," "Grammar in the Freshman Course," "Administration of the Composition Course," among others. Indeed, in the workshop "Objectives and Organization of the Composition Course," the lack of systematization was identified as a primary flaw of the course: "The course has lost effectiveness in large part through the acceptance of multiple objectives" ("Objectives" 9). The workshop members included several recommendations in their report that would serve to enforce system and to combat the diffusion of the class through multiple objectives. One of these recommendations involved the group reading of student essays: "During each semester, group reading of themes by the freshman staff should be carried on as often as needed to bring about a general agreement as to grading standards" (11). Another was to require some sort of shared syllabus and texts. While the workshop participants admitted that "the following questions are such that their answers are largely dependent on local circumstances or on the make-up of a particular staff," they nonetheless made it clear that some sort of uniformity was essential. They thus posed the question "Should there be a detailed syllabus for the course, or should there be a course outline?" and then followed up with a directive: "One or the other is needed" (11). Similarly, they asked, "Should there be complete or only partial uniformity of texts?" and then explained, "At least partial uniformity is made inevitable if the recommendations contained herein are followed" (11).

In these early workshops, the division between people who were making decisions about how to organize the course and those who were teaching the course is quite noticeable. In a second workshop on the organization of the composition course, the participants pondered the question of teaching load and first offered a general answer: "The load should be sufficiently moderate to allow the instructor to achieve our objectives" ("Report" 12). While this group recognized that teaching composition generally requires more labor from the teacher than teaching literature does, their primary concern was not with treating teachers fairly but with improving working conditions so that *administrative* objectives could be met. The subordination of the needs of the worker to the needs of management is a defining characteristic of Keynesian logic. This is not to say that the early members of the CCCC were not teachers of composition. The evidence indicates that most of them had taught and, in some cases, continued to teach composition. But the needs being expressed were not the needs of teachers; rather, they were the needs of a managerial class who wished to control the behavior of teachers.

In addition to systematizing the teaching of composition, the early members of the CCCC were anxious for composition teachers to become consumers of knowledge. In a time when no special training was considered necessary for college teaching, calls were made for the special training of composition teachers, the very teachers who, in the hierarchy of English departments, received the lowest pay and prestige. In one report from a 1950 CCCC workshop, the participants recommended, "College staffs should be allowed to prescribe methods courses, to include educational and psychological breadth, for their own instructors in composition and communication. It is firmly believed that only responsive, trained personnel should be given the privilege of teaching freshman composition" ("Articulating" 38). This passage reveals an argumentative move common in contemporary composition studies: the contingent status of composition teaching is subverted by introducing the warrant that composition teaching is a privilege. And if teaching composition is a privilege, then it makes sense to distinguish the worthy from the unworthy by insisting upon special training. However, neither the unsupported warrant of privilege nor the under-argued claim concerning the need for methods courses address the lack of economic privilege that teachers suffered.

Increasingly, then, composition teachers came to be figured as workers charged with producing a certain outcome—good writing— for students. In order to effectively produce good writing, workers did not need better working conditions so much as better training and management. The pressing question was not how to deal with the division of labor in the teaching of English or how to address the material disadvantages for composition teachers but what knowledge and what kind of supervision composition teachers "needed."

By not addressing the material conditions of composition teaching, the founding members of the CCCC were thus participating in a class process. Rather than asking how to improve the working conditions for teachers, how to make it possible for teachers to have greater autonomy and greater professional advancement, they asked the question of how to extract the proper kind of labor from them. Moved affectively by their own concerns for students as well as by their perception of disorderedly teachers, they set out to establish bureaucratic norms for composition teaching.

# 3

## You Say You Want a Revolution? Managed Universities, Managerial Affects

WHEN DID THE FIELD OF RHETORIC and composition studies begin? As I've indicated in the previous chapter, a number of early histories explicitly rejected the founding of the CCCC as the moment of origin. As more and more histories of the field began to appear in the 1980s and 1990s, this question of origins fueled debate. Does the field go back to the ancient Greeks? To the establishment of a college writing requirement in the late nineteenth century? To sometime in the middle to late twentieth century?

Whenever and wherever they locate the "origin" point, most scholars would agree that something significant happened in the 1960s and into the 1970s. Perhaps as a result of this general agreement, a number of recent histories have looked back to the 1960s as a moment of particular potential, when the field was not yet fully formed and when the possibilities for alternate paths were present and yet untaken (see, for instance, Parks; J. Rice; Sirc). While the 1960s surely did offer new options for composition professionals, the continuation of managerial and normalizing imperatives was certainly just as operative. This chapter will take the founding of the Council of Writing Program Administrators in the 1970s as an instructive moment for illustrating this discipline-wide tension between the quest for potential and the urge toward normalization and order.

It has been relatively easy for the field of composition studies to collectively forget the extent to which the founding of the CCCC represented an effort to normalize the teaching of first-year composition. The prehistory of composition studies, in the years before that founding, has most often been sloughed off with the "current-traditional" label, so that most all of what came before the heroic reemergence of rhetoric in the mid-twentieth century has been too easily dismissed as a formalistic, mechanistic writing pedagogy.[1] This much-disparaged pedagogy of composition lore, as I suggested in chapter 1, is figured as akin to the work of secretaries and so hardly appropriate for introducing students to what James Berlin calls the "overwhelming array of new ideas and new ways of thinking" encountered by "beginning students" in college and with which "the rhetorical training they bring with them inevitably proves . . . unequal to the task of dealing" (*Rhetoric and Reality* 3).

It has been easy, in other words, to see the past as monolithic, as either a dark age of overly rigid, misguided pedagogy or, more recently, as one of open possibility. In fact, a number of recent histories of composition studies have tended toward seeing normalization as a much more recent phenomenon and so have identified exceptional moments from the 1960s and 1970s that might inspire and revivify the field out of its current stagnation. In the late 1960s, without a doubt, composition studies felt the impact of that decade's social and cultural movements. Stephen Parks has sought to recover the "class politics" of the time by tracing the history of the CCCC Students' Right to Their Own Language document. He rejects the very idea of "the traditional and narrow conception of the 'academic professional'" offered by such historians as Berlin and seeks to recover a time "before composition studies was able to slide its participants into academic categories" (Parks 16). For Parks, the late 1960s "represent the moment before it was possible to have an academic career in composition studies" (16).

While drawing more from aesthetic movements than from political ones, Geoffrey Sirc similarly opens *English Composition as a Happening*, his nostalgic and deeply affecting paean to "radical sixties pedagogy," by figuring that same bygone era as one of open possibility: "But what about that *other scene* of writing instruction? Where has that gone, the idea of the writing classroom as blank canvas, ready to be inscribed as a singular compositional space?" (1). Where are they now, Sirc asks, those revolutionary teachers of yore and those classrooms unmarked by norms and outcomes? His conclusion: "Something questionable happened in our field in the late seventies and early eighties: our insecurity over our status as a valid academic field led us to entrench ourselves firmly in professionalism" (6). Professionalism, it seems, killed off those more radical teachers, as we in the field "purged ourselves of any trace of kookiness" in favor of "the trappings of traditional academia" (7).

And yet, despite the richly detailed and professionally inspiring counter-histories that both Parks and Sirc offer, each makes the assumption that "the composition professional" didn't exist in the late 1960s, even though a professional organization for just such a person had existed for nearly two decades by that time. Indeed, in a chapter reflecting on the era of punk, Sirc (perhaps just a bit tongue-in-cheek) asks, "Shouldn't we be surprised that *CCC* of 1977–1980, when it had ample time to hit, didn't give any attention whatsoever to the revolutionary era of the popular that was Punk?" and, after further exposing its absence, concludes, "*CCC* 1977, then, means no fun" (Sirc 236, 250).

This year of "no fun," as it happens, marked the founding year of a new organization for composition professionals, the Council of Writing Program Administrators (WPA). Given the history I've traced so far, a history of the field of composition studies that demonstrates the increasing importance of normalization, of managerial imperatives toward systematization, my shorthand reply to Sirc's question "Shouldn't we be surprised?" would be no. No, we shouldn't be surprised that late 1970s' composition studies tended more toward the establishment of norms than toward the breaking of rules. Rather, what seems more surprising is that composition professionals felt, some twenty-five years after the founding of the CCCC, the need for a new organization devoted exclusively to administration. After all, as the previous chapter demonstrated, the CCCC itself had come into being to meet the needs of composition professionals, which more often than not meant administrators rather than simply teachers. Something clearly must have changed in the field by 1977, and it was something other than a turn toward professionalization. The year 1977, then, marks an important moment in the field, a turn both toward and away from administrative work.

Moreover, the punk years that Sirc cites, 1977–80, also coincide with the beginning of a groundswell as new graduate programs in rhetoric and composition began to proliferate. Of the sixty-five graduate programs listed in *Rhetoric Review*'s 1999 survey, only eight report founding dates before 1977 ("Doctoral Programs"). During the four-year period 1977–80, fourteen programs, or almost a quarter of all currently existing graduate programs in rhetoric and composition, were founded. The time that Sirc labels the beginning of "no fun," in other words, is also the time that the academic discipline commonly known as rhetoric and composition studies fully emerged.

Of course, even before this turn in the late 1970s, neither composition studies nor the culture at large was an open field for activism or aesthetics. The decade of the 1960s was as notable for the growth of management in American society in general and in universities in particular as for countercultural movements. The growth of universities after World War II sparked a major shift in their structure as greater complexity led to greater administrative oversight. Clark Kerr, president of the University of California system during its period of rapid growth in the 1960s, famously coined the term "multiversity" in his 1963 *Uses of the University* to name this changing institution held together by ever increasing numbers of administrators. And although, looking back on the previous decade in 1973, management guru Peter Drucker announced that the management boom that emerged after World War II had ended by 1970, the very idea of management continued to loom large in American society.[2] Drucker himself first published his own thick treatise, *Management: Tasks, Responsibilities, Practices*, in 1973. Just a few years later, in the same year as the founding of the WPA, business historian Alfred Chandler published his now canonical history of management, *The Visible Hand: The Managerial Revolution in American Business*. At the same time, the New Left increasingly published critical accounts of management. Barbara Ehrenreich and John Ehrenreich's well-known definition of the "professional-managerial class," also first appearing in 1977, is one example, as is Harry Braverman's classic castigation of the effects of management in *Labor and Monopoly Capital: The Degradation of Work in the Twentieth Century*, published in 1974. In 1976, Richard

Ohmann, taking a cue from Braverman, published a leftist critique of the institutions shaping "the transmission of literacy and culture" (3–4). His picture of the humanities in general and the composition classroom in particular "around 1965" is less hopeful than the more recent nostalgic views of Parks and Sirc. Ohmann reports feeling that "while teaching undergraduates, and then being an academic administrator," a "gap existed between what we said we were doing . . . and what we were actually achieving. I found it harder to believe that Humanity was being served well by the academic humanities, as our official dogma held, or that the professional apparatus we had invented was a rational structure and not a Rube Goldberg machine" (5). Composition was singled out for special attention and critique in Ohmann's book, occupying a three-chaptered section titled "English 101 and the Military-Industrial Complex," with a central chapter equating "Freshman Composition and Administered Thought."

The 1970s, then, represent for composition studies not so much a time when the counterculture of the previous decade was overthrown. Rather, in both the 1960s and the 1970s, the counterculture existed alongside the increasingly "visible hand" of management. The founding of the CCCC, I argued in the previous chapter, marks the emergence of an increased attention not simply to teaching but also to the more prominent function of the managerial composition professional—or, to use Ehrenreich and Ehrenreich's language, the composition professional-managerial class. The founding of the WPA in 1977, like the founding of the CCCC almost three decades earlier, similarly marks a potentially paradoxical attention to administration even as the discourse suggests a preferred identity as "teacher." Because the CCCC had been drifting toward a focus on research about rhetoric and writing pedagogy, the CCCC of the 1960s had tended to obscure and so to "forget" the administrative role that composition professionals typically perform. By forming a new organization apart from (indeed, not even affiliated with) the CCCC, the WPA simultaneously represented itself as something separate from the work of the scholars of rhetoric and pedagogy in the CCCC, even as this new group similarly privileged teaching over managerial functions.

While these might seem to be contradictory developments, the increasing importance of administration in mid- to late-twentieth-century universities helps to clarify the apparent paradox. The administratively heavy multiversity is, according to Kerr, "powered by money" and so has come to depend more and more on the grant-seeking potential of research (and to be renamed by its critics the "managed" or "corporate" university).[3] Administration, the function pursued by the WPA, and research, the work increasingly valued by the CCCC, represent the twin pillars of the contemporary university. Teaching may remain sentimentally privileged and foregrounded by both organizations (as well as by universities themselves), but the *professional identities* of their members often exceed teaching.

This sentimental foregrounding of teaching, moreover, points to the fundamental role of affect in the history of composition studies (see also Micciche). If the *CCC* of 1977 was, according to Sirc, "no fun," it was nonetheless driven by an emotional attachment to the perceived virtues of teaching and thus an effort to downplay the managerial. This chapter explores that era of "no fun" and the emotions and economics that drove it, situating the founding of the WPA in the context of the expanding, administratively heavy and program-building multiversity. As the CCCC moved toward research *not* focused on the administration of programs, a new organization was made necessary for the growing numbers of administrators taking charge of growing numbers of programs. This separation of the CCCC and a proto-WPA at the very moment that social and ideological issues were coming into the discourse of composition studies may help to explain the repression of the managerial in the field's collective consciousness. Moreover, an affective habit of understanding oneself as a teacher and teaching as inherently good, paired with a general humanist and leftist distrust for management, has tended to establish a kind of boundary for critical inquiry. By substituting the emotionally preferred "teaching" for the more aversive "managing," even when very overtly discussing administrative work, the WPA has continued the obscuring of the managerial function that the CCCC began.

## THE UNIVERSITY OF THE ADMINISTRATOR

I argued in the previous chapter that the founding of the CCCC marked the overt emergence of the composition managerial professional, a class *function* of overseeing the production and appropriation of the surplus value of teaching composition. It should not be surprising, then, to find that the early years of the CCCC, an organization founded largely by administrators, correspond to the early years of administratively heavy "multiversities." Kerr's "multiversity" is very much a postmodern institution—an institution that, unlike the traditional university, has no center: "The university started as a single community—a community of masters and students. It may even be said to have had a soul in the sense of a central animating principle. Today the large American university is, rather, a whole series of communities and activities held together by a common name, a common governing board, and related purposes" (1). As a system, then—a corporate "mechanism" rather than a corporate "body"—the multiversity depends upon *administration* to hold it together. It is, in other words, the university not primarily of the student body or the faculty but of the administrator:

> The general rule is that the administration everywhere becomes, by force of circumstances if not by choice, a more prominent feature of the university. As the institution becomes larger, administration becomes more formalized and separated as a distinct function; as the institution becomes more complex, the role of administration becomes more central in integrating it; as it becomes more related to the once external world, the administration assumes the burdens of these relationships. The managerial revolution has been going on also in the university. (Kerr 28)

It is this managerial "revolution" in the university that was underway during the early years of the CCCC and that, in fact, the CCCC was part of. An affiliate of the National Council of *Teachers* of English, the CCCC came very close to being named "American Association of *Directors* of Freshman English" (see Bird 37; emphasis added). Expanding universities necessarily led to growing numbers of students in required first-year classes, putting more pressure on and thus giving more prominence to the directors of these classes.

But what does it mean for a university to undergo a "managerial revolution"? For one thing, it means that the managerial function becomes more visible. If systematic management was somewhat covertly at work as writing programs emerged (as outlined in chapter 1), new permutations of systematization became ever more overt. One of the dominant systems of administrative oversight in the mid-twentieth century put a premium on the establishment of programs and thus on the increase of administrative control. "Planning Programming Budgeting System," a management strategy first used by the federal government and then inconsistently transferred to higher education during the 1960s and 1970s, "required the identification and classification of all activities into discrete programs," programs that "were to be stated in objectives and outcomes" (Birnbaum 35, 39). It seems more than a coincidence that positions to lead writing *programs*, including basic writing *programs* and writing-across-the-curriculum *programs*, began to proliferate during this period.

Indeed, as we know from the recent history of composition, the late 1960s and early 1970s saw a boomlet in the proliferation of writing programs and writing centers. In part, this growth was fueled by open admissions programs and back-to-basics movements. While generally aligned with student protests, open admissions and basic writing programs were also very much part of systematic management and budgeting strategies. Moreover, as Bruce Horner and others have argued, apart from the program that Mina Shaughnessy famously led at City College, most basic writing programs show little evidence of being aligned with open admissions, much less with student protests (see Horner, "Discoursing"; Strickland, "Errors"; Ritter). If anything, they seem often to have been prompted by a conservative emphasis on returning to the "basics" of education (see Trimbur). What is often overlooked in traditional histories of composition, further, is that the discourse that set this so-called democratization in motion—that is, the discourse of access—also set in motion various administrative structures. Many new basic writing programs emerged, and new directors were hired to lead writing labs or centers that would offer tutorial services for these at-risk students (see Strickland, "Making the Managerial Conscious"; Gunner, "Doomed"). In fact, in addition to the changes in the CCCC that I will detail below, the other major change that happened with administration of first-year writing was the shift from the directing of *classes* to the directing of *programs*.[4]

This setting in motion of administrative structures to, on the face of it, meet the needs of students who would not otherwise have had access to a college education marks an important condition of possibility of the field of composition studies.[5] It is the moment when material conditions made it possible to begin to offer doctoral degrees in composition and rhetoric in the 1970s and 1980s: people who could direct first-year writing programs, basic writing programs, writing-across-the-curriculum programs, and writing centers were suddenly in demand. As Ohmann has related in an introduction to his *English in America*, the job prospects for PhDs in literature had bottomed out by the late 1960s. Increasing numbers of newly minted literature PhDs, then, took jobs in writing program administration.

In fact, such large numbers took these jobs that a new organization formed to meet the needs of this group: the Council of Writing Program Administrators. As should be clear from previous chapters, it isn't that no one was in charge of first-year composition courses before 1977. English departments routinely appointed someone within their ranks to oversee composition courses and to train graduate teaching assistants. However, before the proliferation of new kinds of writing programs, it tended to be the case that an experienced professor (as in the case of George Wykoff at Purdue) would take on the job. With the new writing programs, *brand-new* professors increasingly were hired specifically to work as administrators.

## RESEARCH IMPERATIVES AND CULTURAL SHIFTS IN THE CCCC

The WPA, it might be said, emerged as the return of the repressed. As demonstrated in the last chapter, the CCCC had been organized in 1949 with an agenda very similar to the WPA's. In other words, had the CCCC remained an organization primarily devoted to questions directly relevant to the directing of writing programs, it seems that the formation of the WPA would have been a redundancy. But by 1959, when the CCCC leadership considered a name change, the idea of administration was no longer emphasized; indeed, out of ten suggested names, not one mentioned administration.[6]Edward P. J. Corbett locates this shift in a turn toward rhetoric, which, as he describes it, offered "real professionalization of the writing teacher":

> [A]t the 1961 4Cs convention in Washington, DC, a workshop was offered under the title "Rhetoric—the Neglected Art." Then at the 1963 4Cs convention in Los Angeles, rhetoric suddenly burst on the scene. Several of the panels and workshops at that meeting bore the word rhetoric in their title, and in the October issue of *College Composition and Communication* (*CCC*) that year, the editor, Ken Macrorie, published seven of the papers under the special title "Toward a New Rhetoric." The first Scholars Seminar sponsored by the 4Cs met in December of 1964 at Denver under the leadership of Robert Gorrell, and the subject was rhetoric. The reports of that seminar were published in the October 1965 issue of CCC under the special title "Further Toward a New Rhetoric." (69)

This shift away from administrative issues was also signaled by William Irmscher's decision as editor of *CCC*, beginning in 1965, to

> reduce the number of articles which described the organization of freshman English programs, the training of teaching assistants, and procedures for grading papers. . . . He wanted it to become the major periodical for non-fiction studies, publishing rhetorical studies, stylistic analyses, and thematic and critical treatments of great essayists. Additionally, it would "serve as a miscellany for articles on the relationship between language and composition, grammar and composition, and literature and composition." (Bird 111)

In short, a new generation of CCCC leaders was moving the focus of the organization away from the administration of first-year composition courses and onto the study of language and pedagogy more generally.

As a result, as more new PhDs with specializations in literature found themselves responding to ads for positions in writing program administration published in the newly established Modern Language Association (MLA) job information list, and as people like Kenneth Bruffee and Mina Shaughnessy found themselves in charge of newly ubiquitous basic writing programs, they began asking questions that people in NCTE and the CCCC "had never heard of" (Bruffee qtd. in Heckathorn 215)—or, more precisely, questions that people in the CCCC had ceased emphasizing.

Administration, in other words, became something of a secret, or, at least, a secondary identity for composition professionals already firmly networked into the CCCC. It could be inferred that administration was not considered a sufficiently "intellectual" enterprise by this generation of CCCC leaders, that the proper study of composition professionals should be writing itself, not the training of teachers of writing. But, of course, the training of writing teachers did not go away; rather, it became the unspoken motivation for the study of writing. In addition, the segmenting of administrative issues away from the CCCC did not mean that people were not involved in both organizations; in fact, Edward Corbett, program chair of the 1970 CCCC Convention, was initially elected to head the new WPA organization, though he declined to take that position (see Heckathorn 216).

This shift toward the scholarship of writing and rhetoric also signals a shift enforced by the multiversity, a shift toward further sharpening the division between teaching and research. As a number of writers have shown, the multiversity—"powered by money," in the words of Clark Kerr—has increasingly looked to faculty research as a source of revenue. With the diminishing of federal and state support that has continued over the last half-century, universities have become, in the words of Sheila Slaughter and Larry L. Leslie, among others, entrepreneurial: encouraging and rewarding grant writing, taking a mandatory cut from all grants for the use of the university. Given the potential for increased revenue from research, greater emphasis has been placed on research that might bring in grants and other types of funding. As a result, less money has gone to the support of teaching or even to research on teaching, and so research has tended to drift away from pedagogy.

In addition to this trend toward identifying themselves increasingly with inquiry into writing itself, CCCC members were responding to social movements, bringing questions of ideology and activism to bear on the teaching of writing. In 1970, for example, a number of resolutions on social issues were brought to the CCCC business meeting, including a Resolution on Women, a Resolution on Political Oppression, an Anti-Colonialism Resolution, and an Anti-War Resolution (CCCC Preliminary Program). And as Stephen Parks chronicles, in 1974, after years of debate, the Students' Right to Their Own Language document was approved at a convention with the theme "Hidden Agendas: What Are We Doing When We Do What We Do?" Strictly administrative issues, in other words, were taking a back burner as the world changed and interests of CCCC members broadened.

This boundary work was happening, moreover, at the same time that graduate programs in rhetoric and composition were emerging. As a result, at the very moment that it became possible to study rhetoric and composition, whether in special postgraduate programs or in newly formed graduate concentrations, the research of the field was less about the administration of programs and more about rhetoric and pedagogy. These new research-oriented programs, then, even when led by the same people who were directing undergraduate writing programs, were focused on teaching the writing process and rhetoric much more than on addressing administrative issues. (Indeed, as Jeanne Gunner has recently pointed out, there seems to still be "anxious discourse on the value of WPA courses in graduate composition programs" [274].) My point here is not to condemn PhD programs in rhetoric and composition for attending to matters of invention and process but rather to point out the dissociation, the division, that erupted. This division, I argue, marks the moment of emergence of the WPA as a separate organization—as well as the moment of emergence of rhetoric and composition studies as an increasingly recognized field of study. In other words, there was an odd splitting at the very moment that the field of rhetoric and composition studies was becoming recognized, a conceptual and practical break between the work of studying writing and rhetoric in general and the work of directing writing programs.

## THE INTELLECTUAL WORK OF
## MANAGEMENT IN THE EARLY WPA

The WPA, then, emerged as a way to forge a new group identity for those who found themselves somewhat unexpectedly thrust into administrative roles. One of the important functions of the WPA was offering space for the development of a collective consciousness, a sense that writing program administrators were a group with common concerns. This function emerges very clearly in the pages of the early *WPA Newsletter*, which quickly became a journal, *WPA: Writing Program Administration*. For the early members of the WPA, writing program administration was a new area of expertise. Thus, despite the fact that people had been supervising first-year writing for years, and despite the fact that the CCCC was originally founded to meet the needs of that group, Kenneth Bruffee and other early founders expressed their sense that the field was new. In part, Bruffee's editorials and other contributions to the WPA journal were doing boundary work, establishing the domain of professional expertise: "Through the association and its journal, our particular goal is to serve English studies, the humanities, and postsecondary education in general by defining and contributing to this new field of expertise. In doing so, WPA and its journal testify to the fact that WPAs have begun to develop for themselves a sense of professional identity" (Bruffee, "Editorial" [1980] 7). Indeed, the idea of a "new field of expertise" makes sense in that this field had emerged through the cutting away of administration from the central concerns of the CCCC.

From almost the beginning, moreover, the leaders in this new field of expertise regarded their work as an area of scholarly inquiry, not simply a skill. In support of this view, the *WPA Newsletter* quickly became a journal and, from the outset, was refereed. Year after year, Bruffee, the organization's first president and the journal's first editor, reminded readers and potential contributors of this distinction:

"Because the articles we publish have been read and approved by a panel of knowledgeable and respected people in the field, publication in the WPA Newsletter can be cited with confidence on our authors' curriculum vitae" ("Editorial" [1978b] 3). Indeed, he noted, "*WPA* is one of the few refereed, national academic publications concerned with writing" ("Editorial" [1980] 7). In a recent interview, Bruffee recalls how and why he made the decision early on to make offering a reputable forum for the intellectual work of WPAs an early and central concern of the organization:

> I found out by going to a meeting of journal editors at MLA that they were talking about the difference between refereed and non-refereed journals—one counted and the other one didn't. I said, "OK, if we want to count, we'll make it refereed." And we put on people from Yale and Harvard so that we had some fancy names on there, and it looked good. The whole idea was to give it that quality so that people who were publishing in it could say, "This goes on—this refereed journal goes on the resume." So it's legitimized in that way. (qtd. in Heckathorn 217)

In other words, providing a space to indeed legitimize the intellectual work of writing program administrators—to give it a space for public dissemination and professional approval—was an important means of distinguishing the work of the writing program administrator from the work of the composition teacher/scholar.

Although the WPA has recently made much of a distinction between "intellectual work" and "management activity," the early WPA clearly asked intellectual questions about management activity. The questions were, without a doubt, questions of management: How do we assure quality programs? How do we compete with the rest of the English department and other departments and programs for funds? One of the earliest initiatives of the WPA was very much a professional/managerial undertaking: the establishment of the consultant-evaluator service, funded by a grant from the Exxon Education Foundation. Begun by 1979, it shortly thereafter achieved national recognition (and continues to be a popular service offered by the organization). Harvey Weiner reported in 1981, for example, that "the high quality of the WPA consultant-evaluator training program" had led to an invitation to "to discuss our procedures with the National Endowment for the Humanities" (7).

Assessment of programs, then, has from the outset been a central concern of the WPA. For some, addressing this concern meant turning to corporate models, thus erasing for all practical purposes any supposed distinction between academic "administration" and business "management." William F. Woods, for example, advocated the investigation of industrial management for possible models: "How should we administer these evaluation programs? . . . [I]f there is talk about 'managing' our departments, we might as well investigate the techniques that industrial managers, in fact, use to evaluate their own personnel" (9). For Woods, turning to management strategies used by industry was necessary for dealing with economic crises that characterized the 1970s (and, to a large extent, continue to beset higher education); decreasing funding suggested to him the need to intervene more directly into teachers' work[7]: "As our economic crisis deepens and enrollments continue to fall, good teaching becomes ever more crucial. The real question, therefore, is not, can we afford to include in our budgets the cost of what industry would call 'quality-control procedures.' The real question is, can we afford not to?" (15).

Writing programs, in short, cost money. With the tendency toward small class sizes and the ubiquity of anywhere from one to three or four required courses in a given institution, they required a good deal of money to hire teachers (while "saving" money, as we know, by hiring more and more part-timers as well as graduate students to teach these courses and thereby setting up the class process of appropriating the surplus labor of these teachers). According to Kerr, the multiversity that sponsors these programs "is more a mechanism—a series of processes producing a series of results—a mechanism held together by administrative rules and powered by money" (20). This reduction to management and economics rather downplays the role of people working in programs, suggesting that the administration of programs in the multiversity hardly involves affect of any kind.

But if the various parts of the multiversity are powered by money, then conflict occurs when the parts have to compete for funding, and conflict certainly stirs up human emotions. The abysmally poor economic climate of the 1970s contributed to a very poor job market for English PhDs. At the same time that traditional faculty jobs were scarce, there was an increase, as mentioned earlier, in the hiring of faculty who could direct writing programs. The competition for resources in departments that were losing tenure lines in literature often led to a sense of embattlement among these newly minted administrators. Reporting on a WPA workshop in 1982, Stephen Zelnick explained: "What emerged [at the workshop in 1982] was a list of concerns that reflect the daily intricacies by which WPAs tend to be ensnared. Foremost on this list was 'asserting the place of writing on the campus.' This, in most cases, turned out to mean 'battling the English departments for support and recognition'" (11).

These economic difficulties, which seemed to threaten administrators' abilities to assure quality programs, led to concerns about hiring. In particular, many expressed concern over how to guard against hiring composition teachers who were not qualified to teach composition—a concern that echoes the distinction Wykoff made in 1939 between composition teachers and composition colleagues. Robert R. Bataille, for example, in a 1980 *WPA* article, declared "hiring faculty who are truly competent to teach writing" to be "one of the most serious problems any writing program administrator or department chair faces today" (17). Bataille recognized that "times are hard" economically, but rather than seeing this from the standpoint of labor, it is (logically) defined as a managerial problem: WPAs must be especially wary when hiring. People who are not really devoted to composition may try to pass themselves off as composition specialists; Bataille thus offers tips on how to distinguish the fraud from the real thing. The economic difficulties, for directors, suggested a threat to their programs and thus their own livelihoods more than it clarified for them the effects it had on the people teaching the course, especially given that part-time faculty were rarely paid a truly living wage without becoming overloaded with classes and, moreover, rarely enjoyed benefits of health care or retirement.

By asking questions about the hiring of writing teachers, the early leadership of the WPA touched upon an issue that very much continues to confound the profession today: how to respond to "the problems of part-time faculty and issues raised by the increased use of part-time instructors throughout our profession" (Weiner 7). The increased use of part-time faculty was and continues to be an effect of the multiversity as it morphed into what more recent critics call the entrepreneurial university (see Slaughter and Leslie). The multiversity, as a complex institution, set up the need for increasing numbers of administrators. As federal funding began to evaporate toward the end of the 1970s and continuing to the present, a heavier emphasis on research fed the development of PhD programs and research that wasn't necessarily connected to either administration or teaching.

Clearly, then, the work of writing program administration is *managerial* work. That doesn't mean that it is not simultaneously *intellectual* work. Managerial work does require intellectual labor. To ask questions about the management of teachers is as much an intellectual activity as is developing a curriculum. In fact, developing a curriculum for others to implement is itself a management activity—it is a putting into place of structures to guide the work of others. Despite the fact that some WPAs have been comfortable acknowledging the managerial function of writing program administration work, the dominant discourse of the WPA council has tended to push aside that association. As I'll demonstrate in the following section, the managerial function was reconceptualized as "teaching."

### MANAGERIAL AVERSIONS

The WPA, then, took up intellectual questions related to managerial functions—how to hire the best workers, how to assess the quality of programs. At the same time, almost from the beginning of the organization, the WPA discourse showed an aversion toward so-called managerial tasks. In a move reminiscent of the early CCCC discourse, these administrators identified themselves as teachers. In a talk given at the 1977 MLA convention and reprinted in the first volume of the WPA journal, Bruffee, while explaining "the purpose of WPA to our colleagues, some of whom have expressed doubt about the necessity and goals of such an organization," described a growing need for "leadership" among "writing teachers" ("Editorial" [1978a] 6). Such an organization was necessary because of "a striking change [that] has taken place in the organization and visibility of what we writing teachers do" (7). The change to which he refers is "the fast-growing tendency in colleges and universities throughout the country to involve whole campuses in writing programs" (7). Because "writing is no longer perceived as the exclusive province, responsibility, and tough luck of the English department" but "as the active concern of the whole college," "the writing program at many schools has been catapulted into a new, important, demanding, and highly visible position of leadership" (7–8).

Writing teachers, transformed in these passages from people into writing *programs*, now found themselves taking on new roles. While occupying an important new leadership role, WPAs, according to Bruffee, remained a beleaguered group: "The profession is in the habit of considering them second-class citizens, in part because they have stepped through the looking glass . . . into that never-never land where croquet mallets turn into flamingoes and croquet balls turn into hedgehogs: the land of administration; and mainly, of course, because they take the job of teaching writing seriously" (9). Writing program administrators have stepped into the upside-down "land of administration," which Bruffee equates with an affective stance toward the teaching of writing: the taking of it seriously.

Bruffee goes on to describe other causes for this beleaguered state: WPAs get blamed for the deplorable state of student writing; most are untenured and thus vulnerable; most are just out of graduate programs and have not been trained to teach writing or to administer programs (9, 10). What's especially interesting here is the martyred affective stance assigned to WPAs: important but misunderstood, they feel bad. Even so, they have an essential task: creating a *space* to manage the affect that most everyone else attaches to writing.

Our students cannot learn how to write in a context in which the general public, legislators, college administrators, college faculty, most English departments, and, alas, even many writing teachers fear writing, view writing as punishment, and have an understanding of the nature of language which is roughly at the level of a "grammar quiz" on the inner pages of *Readers Digest*. (11)

And, says Bruffee, it is the need to teach others, to counter these affective stances through a process of education, that makes WPAs something other than managers:

> [I]n my list of what writing program administrators are expected to do I have not included what most of us think administrators do—the managerial tasks of making up schedules, assigning classes, hiring and firing, that sort of thing. Of course some writing program administrators have those responsibilities too. But where writing program administrators differ—or should differ—from most other college administrators is that the most important part of their job is not managerial but directly educational. . . . In fact, I would say that only when writing program administrators conceive of their job in this larger way, as teaching, do they have a prayer of doing the job as it must be done. (12)

Here again, while acknowledging the possibility of some "managerial tasks," Bruffee distinguishes such tasks from teaching, which, he says, is the true function of the writing program administrator.[8]

The figure of the "teacher-administrator" remained a central figure in the early WPA discourse, representing at least Bruffee's sense of writing program administration. If part of the WPA council's concern recently has been to define writing program administration as intellectual work, against purely "managerial" work, much of the early WPA's efforts were concentrated in distinguishing this work as a form of teaching. In a 1979 editorial, for example, Bruffee asserted: "Most writing program administrators continue to be writing teachers, differing from other writing teachers only in the nature of the people we teach. We teach not only college and university students, but often other college and university teachers as well. We administer in part *by* teaching. We teach in part *through* administration" (7). And in an article appearing the following year, Walter Jewell argued that "administrators must find ways to define their role, to themselves as well as to the academic community at large, as educators rather than simply as managers" (9). For Bruffee, the emphasis on teaching no doubt stemmed in part from his own particular experience as the "first Director of Freshman English at Brooklyn College—the Open Admissions Director" (qtd. in Heckathorn 214). Noting in a recent interview that the job of writing program administrator "differs from institution to institution," he explained the nature of his own position: "At my institution the chair controlled the budget and scheduled the courses; my job was more of a teaching job. . . . It had to be a kind of large persuasive role—an organizational role" (qtd. in Heckathorn 215). Here, "an organizational role" is equated with teaching, though it is certainly a managerial function.

This very overt substitution of the more benign, or even laudatory, "teaching" for the "managerial" or even "administrative" suggests that maybe the managerial isn't so unconscious, after all: as Slavoj Žižek would put it, we know what we're doing, and we're doing it anyway! What seems unconscious, however, is the affective weight of "teaching." Teaching seems to carry with it a sense of benign importance, or even of moral goodness. If, as administrators, we're still teachers, then we escape the traditional humanistic and the new leftist critiques of management.

But teaching is a technology like any other—a technology that does not by itself carry value. Lynn Worsham draws from Pierre Bourdieu and Jean-Claude Passeron to distinguish a neutral sense of "pedagogy" as such from dominant pedagogy, with the latter referring to "the power held by dominant discourses to impose the legitimate mode of conception and perception" (221). According to Worsham, "The main task of any society is to create the social desire to cooperate and unite with others and to organize the social energy by identifying the appropriate objects, aims, and persons for emotional attachments and by prohibiting others as legitimate loci of interest" (223). The default work of pedagogy, in other words, is the work of normalization, work that imposes itself by establishing proper "emotional attachments." In this way, pedagogy does turn out to be quite a bit like management, in that both tend toward normalization and both work at the affective level.

But like pedagogy, management need not necessarily be "dominant management," which seeks to normalize without consideration of the human toll of such a process. Insofar as the early discourse of the WPA embraced the administrative role apart from teaching, that discourse often tended toward defining it differently, as a humanistic pursuit rather than what Clark Kerr saw as a mechanistic one. Hand-in-hand with his concern to define WPAs as teacher-administrators was Bruffee's recurring effort to define administration as humanistic: "To understand writing program administration as fully as possible is . . . a humanistic pursuit of the highest importance" (Bruffee [1980] 7). Jewell also speaks to this ideal of a higher pursuit, calling for administrators to see their position not primarily in terms of professional advancement but in terms of service to others: "To be employed as a teacher and administrator is not the same thing as *being* a teacher and administrator. To do that, one must define one's role in terms of service to education rather than in terms of rewards emanating from position" (12).

At the same time that Bruffee was keen to define administration as a humanistic pursuit, he nonetheless made clear that administrative work required a kind of knowledge distinct from traditional text-based scholarship in the humanities:

> Most techniques required for faculty development . . . or for any other aspect of administrative leadership, are not to be found in the carrels of the Huntington Library or the Folger. We might begin to find some of that knowledge and expertise, though, by studying strategies of organizational change, small group work, and the nature of bureaucracy and institutional structure. ("Editorial" [1980] 8)

While they might share with members of NCTE and the CCCC a focus on teaching, the early WPA leaders nonetheless were careful to distinguish the kind of teaching they did from the teaching of writing. As editor of the journal, Bruffee explained:

Although teaching composition is certainly relevant to what WPAs do, *WPA* is less likely to publish articles on how to teach composition than articles on how to deal with composition teachers, less likely to publish articles on how to put a curriculum to good use in the classroom than articles on how to get a faculty to design a good curriculum and how to get that curriculum put to good use in many classrooms. ("Editorial" [1980] 9)

Zelnick, reporting on the 1982 WPA workshop, also noted this distinction: "Unlike most writing conferences, the workshop (on the administration of writing programs, 1982) did not cover such familiar ground as the writing process or theories of language acquisition but focused on program design and evaluation, and administrative problems" (11).

These definitions, then, functioned, on the one hand, to distinguish the work of writing program administration from managerial work, a concern that continues to inform the more recent "Intellectual Work" document. On the other hand, they also divided the work of administering writing programs from the work of teaching writing. Even if administration was a form of teaching, and even if it was a humanistic pursuit, it nonetheless asked questions that neither the CCCC nor other humanists were asking. In short, the founders of the WPA were asking managerial questions, but they were hoping to avoid the popular humanistic disparaging of "managerial" work, insofar as that work was understood to be mechanistic and nonintellectual. They were, in other words, hoping to avoid an association with mechanical tasks, just as earlier in the century the discourse of teaching writing worked to separate so-called mechanical tasks of writing from more intellectual, creative work.

In his final editorial for the *WPA* journal, Bruffee noted the profound changes that he had witnessed while working as a writing program administrator: "What I have learned about the profession at large is that at the present time it is undergoing profound changes. Ten years ago writing programs were for the most part back room affairs, run on a shoestring. Some may still be. But today most writing programs are increasingly well supported and increasingly recognized as central to the curriculum" ([1983] 11). While they may have felt themselves to be beleaguered, and while they may continue to feel the disappointment of not being able to fully implement what they feel is important, WPAs in 1983, according to Bruffee, enjoyed certain advantages—greater economic stability and increasing recognition. Though averse to the label of management, WPAs benefited from the managed university, experiencing greater support and the attendant affect of "rightness" that accompanies such support.

### MANAGERIAL WORK AS INTELLECTUAL WORK

As the Council of Writing Program Administrators' document "Evaluating the Intellectual Work of Writing Program Administrators" makes clear, the effort to define the work of administration as other than managerial has not let up since the early years of the organization. This document, as described in some detail in the introduction to this book, downplays the "managerial" tasks and seeks to redefine much of the work of administration as intellectual work, requiring research and specialized knowledge.

Of course, administration does require intellectual work. So does management. The two, as I've indicated earlier, are not distinct forms of action: both refer to the supervision and direction of others' work, with "administration" being the preferred name for managers in not-for-profit organizations. And certainly, as indicated in important books published over the last decade, WPAs may well be researchers, theorists, and activists (see the two volumes by Rose and Weiser, as well as Adler-Kassner).

All of these alternate identifications for the writing program administrator, however, may tend to obscure the fundamental reality: WPAs function as managers. The organizational separation of the CCCC from the WPA council, moreover, tends to further obscure the historically shared conditions of emergence of the two. These obscurations and divisions, as Jeanne Gunner argues, tend to "maintain . . . the division of disciplinary work and disciplinary knowledge, and so also maintain the conservative agenda of writing programs by privileging professionalization over cultural engagement" (264).

This "conservative agenda" refers not to the personal politics of any administrator but to the normalizing function of most writing programs (see also Rice, "Conservative," and Banks and Alexander). As the next chapter will demonstrate, even quite progressive personal and pedagogical politics can be undone through an unspoken assumption of the moral imperative of spreading these politics through administrative oversight.

# 4

## Democratic Pedagogies and the Persistence of Control

OVER THE LAST THIRTY YEARS, it has become possible to speak of composition studies as a field of study, as a discipline, as an area of specialization. A person can become a student of rhetoric and composition, something that was hardly possible before the 1980s. Now, however, graduate programs in rhetoric and composition proliferate, and although the academic job market remains constricted for most scholars in the humanities, holders of doctorates in composition studies remain employable. The number of full-time, tenure-track positions in rhetoric and composition almost doubled in the period between 1987 and 1993, according to a study conducted by Stuart Brown, Paul Meyer, and Theresa Enos. And the most recent MLA reports continue to confirm that the number of jobs in rhetoric and composition annually far outnumber jobs in any traditional historical area of literary studies.

The professional and disciplinary growth of rhetoric and composition studies has not gone unnoticed or unremarked upon outside the field. Literary theorist Paul Bové has gone so far as to suggest that an interest in composition studies signifies a kind of crass careerism, asserting that despite the current crisis in English departments, "well-funded specialists in composition and pedagogy" are among those who "feel no anxiety at all" (29). For Bové, a person like Richard Lanham, "whose career began in traditional 'lit. crit.' and moved to the more lucrative areas of composition theory and 'pedagogy,' . . . represents the 'English Studies professional' in America" (163). While Bové seems to dismiss the possible intellectual value of the study of rhetoric and composition, he does nevertheless point to a material reality that scholars in composition studies seem unwilling to critically confront: specialists in composition are in demand.[1]

It is important to acknowledge the material success of composition studies as a discipline in order to get beyond the deeply felt sense (clear in the work of the early WPA organization, as recounted in chapter 3) that composition specialists represent an underclass in English departments. Certainly, composition teachers who are not on the tenure track do occupy a marginal economic position, as do the still too-common untenured writing program administrators. However, composition professionals—tenured faculty who teach undergraduate and graduate courses in rhetoric and composition and who more often than not function as administrators—are firmly ensconced in the central work that fiscally sustains English departments (unless the writing program has declared its independence; see O'Neill, Crow, and Burton). Saying that composition professionals are firmly ensconced is not to deny that competition for resources doesn't still happen or that misunderstandings are not still common. But in terms of job prospects and long-term security, composition professionals continue to do well.

What is curious, then, is that just as composition studies was becoming a more common and more popular field of study within graduate English departments in the 1980s and 1990s, narratives of both its marginal status and of its "radically democratic" potential proliferated. The call for a more radical democracy extended beyond composition studies, as political thinkers made the claim that "the creation of an egalitarian society will entail extending . . . democratic principles into ever expanding areas of daily life: work, education, leisure, the home" (Trend 3). But how do attempts to construct "democratic" and "empowering" forms of pedagogy function in a body of scholarship that is working at the same time to establish the centrality of a normalizing composition studies—a move that is particularly clear in James Berlin's efforts to rearticulate connections between poetics (literary criticism) and rhetorics (text production) while also arguing for a politicized social-epistemic pedagogy?

In this chapter, I will examine the convergence of these two phenomena: the rise of composition studies as an academic discipline and the increasing emphasis within the discipline on the democratic nature of the discipline. I will argue that despite composition studies' theoretical articulations with various forms of leftist thought, the appeal to democracy and the classroom practices that tend to be favored may function instead as articulations of managerial commonplaces, unexamined ideologies and practices that do not always forward democratic goals. In particular, I will show that the appeal to democracy in composition studies has emerged alongside similar appeals to quality and teamwork in corporate management. According to Foucault, channeling Nietzsche, it is the very existence of "class domination" that "generates the idea of liberty" (see Foucault, "Nietzsche" 150). The rise of "liberatory" pedagogies, then, may be connected to—or at least not necessarily in opposition to—managerial hierarchies within the field. Or, to move outside of the language of articulation, liberatory pedagogies may function, through their repetition and ubiquity, to habituate administrators and teachers to a particular affect, making the *effects* then of administrative oversight less visible.

Before I begin this critique, however, I want to make it clear that I do not intend to "discredit" the scholars who have appealed to democracy in their work, to unveil their work for progressive politics to be mere self-aggrandizement or self-deception. Rather, I hope to show the constraints that operate in composition studies and the ways in which even good intentions may not go far enough toward dislodging default tendencies toward class processes of appropriating surplus labor. By mapping out the constraints, I hope to make available the space in which to rethink what it might mean to be an oppositional teacher, intellectual, *and* manager. To this end, I will first offer a brief genealogy of the concept of "democracy" in composition studies in order to demonstrate that it is, like all signifiers, slippery. I will then focus on James Berlin's work, in which the articulations among disciplinarity, democracy, and the postmodern workplace are particularly pronounced. Next, I will look at the postmodern workplace itself, as it is envisioned by exponents of "quality" management, to show how presumably democratic practices are being commodified. Finally, I will consider how appeals to democracy may function to school the emotions of writing teachers.

## A GENEALOGY OF DEMOCRACY IN
## COMPOSITION STUDIES

Although an overtly "political turn" in composition studies emerged most visibly in the 1990s, the appeal to democracy and the possibility of a democratic or "liberatory" form of teaching has appeared sporadically throughout composition's history.[2] In fact, some histories of the teaching of composition (most notably, Berlin's) attempt to create an explicitly democratic lineage for contemporary writing instruction. As Foucault argues, however, the search for origins presupposes "the existence of immobile forms that precede the external world of accident and succession" ("Nietzsche" 142). Against such a misguided search, Foucault offers the Nietzschean concept of "genealogy," which does not seek to "trace the gradual curve of [events'] evolution, but to isolate the different scenes in which they engaged in different roles" (140). The concept of democracy has played a variety of roles in the history of writing instruction. By briefly isolating a few of these roles, I hope to show that even so appealing and generous a concept as democracy can also support a default managerial function of class process.

The emergence of the required course in composition in the nineteenth century tends to be figured as a falling away from a rhetorical tradition of schooling that is said to have prepared students for the practice of public, democratic contestation (Connors, "Rhetoric"; Halloran). In this narrative of decline and fall, the first glimmer of hope of a new, more democratic practice of composition instruction appears with Fred Newton Scott, a professor of rhetoric at the University of Michigan from 1899 to 1926. According to Berlin, Scott's approach to the teaching of composition was "a uniquely American development, a rhetoric for a modern democratic state," and a precursor of social-epistemic rhetoric (*Rhetoric and Reality* 47). Berlin maintains that in emphasizing the "social" uses of writing and speaking, Scott "posed a rhetoric of public service, a system distinguished by its ethical commitment to the public good" (49).

By enshrining Scott as the proponent of a "democratic," socially directed rhetoric, however, Berlin tends, oddly enough, to overlook the social context out of which Scott's ideas were formed. The

Jacksonian version of democracy that emerged early in the nineteenth century was a democracy for white men, many of whom
actively sought to remove the "threat" of Native Americans and
somewhat more passively to encourage the belief that African slaves
were less than human and to relegate white women to a separate,
private sphere removed from work and politics (see Saxton). By the
late 1800s, this version of democracy was being challenged in a number of ways. A series of economic depressions between 1873 and 1896
had eroded confidence in the then-dominant model of the captain
of industry, whose control of the market was giving way to large
corporations (see, for example, Bederman 12). Moreover, immigrant
men and native-born white women were seeking a greater political
voice, challenging the dominance of native-born white middle-class
men (Bederman 13–14). In response to these economic and political crises, a new discourse of "civilization" emerged. According to
cultural historian Gail Bederman, "civilization" was a gendered and
racialized concept deployed around the turn of the century as a way
of reconceptualizing America's—and middle-class white men's—
dominance in the world:

> In the context of the late nineteenth century's popularized
> Darwinism, civilization was seen as an explicitly racial concept.
> It meant more than simply "the west" or "industrially advanced
> societies." Civilization denoted a precise stage in human racial
> evolution. . . . Human races were assumed to evolve from
> simple savagery, through violent barbarism, to advanced and
> valuable civilization. But only white races had, as yet, evolved
> to the civilized stage. (Bederman 25)

In this context, promoting the good of society, as Berlin maintains
Scott's rhetoric does, can be read as promoting the evolution and
ultimate perfection of (white) civilization (see Bederman 26). Indeed,
Scott's keen interest in the social Darwinist Herbert Spencer would
suggest that Scott was not opposed to the idea that society was evolv-
ing and that white people were the most highly evolved (see F. Scott).

Scott's "democratic" rhetoric, then, needs to be understood con-
textually. While Berlin tends to read Scott's lectures and articles as

permutations of current theories of literacy and rhetoric, Kathryn Flannery reads these same works as revealing the limitations of the cultural ideologies within which Scott was working. She finds a definite xenophobic strain in Scott's pedagogical theories and describes his concern as being with the question of "how to civilize, order, and control what might otherwise degenerate into 'error,' defined as deviance from a domestic, native, noble standard" (131). Without a doubt, Scott's ideas about democracy would have been constrained by the time in which he lived, and Flannery's reading of the moment of falsehood in Scott's work is a useful antidote to the laudatory readings of Berlin (and Stewart and Stewart, among others).

After Scott, the second moment in the narrative of progress toward a more democratic pedagogy was the emergence of communication skills courses in the 1940s (see Berlin, *Rhetoric and Reality* 93–104; Crowley, *Composition* 155–86). Emphasizing both writing and speaking, these courses were part of a larger general education movement that gained strength as World War II was building. Advocates of general education argued that "the point of education was the preservation of democracy" (Crowley, *Composition* 162). Toward the end of making the world safe for democracy, participants in a 1950 CCCC workshop described the purpose of the communication course as being "to develop students' abilities to give and receive meanings conveyed in *language*, to the further end that they become effective and alert members of a democratic society" ("Objectives" 15).

These appeals to democracy have led scholars like Berlin to hold up the communication course as a model for progressive pedagogy. But how did "democracy" signify for students and teachers in these communication courses? If the communication course emerged after World War II, it emerged with the Cold War, and "democracy" was thus strongly articulated with capitalism, against communism. This use of democracy as the social form of capitalism would seem at odds with the more leftist articulations of democracy that tend to circulate in contemporary composition studies.

The appeal to political empowerment also circulated widely in the 1970s, in the wake of various social movements. Peter Elbow, for instance, opens *Writing Without Teachers* in this way: "Many people are now trying to become less helpless, both personally and politically: trying to claim more control over their own lives. One of the ways people most lack control over their own lives is through lacking control over words" (vii). Mina Shaughnessy similarly argues for a connection between power over words and power in society in *Errors and Expectations*: "A person who does not control the dominant code of literacy in a society that generates more writing than any society in history is likely to be pitched against more obstacles than are apparent to those who have already mastered that code" (13). These arguments, while representing what have tended to be figured as opposite schools of thought in composition studies (the cultivation of personal voice versus the acquisition of academic literacy), both view the development of writing skills as a pro-democratic act. However, as we know from the research of Harvey Graff and others on the "literacy myth," depending on writing alone to broaden opportunities and thus democratize society is not enough. Graff's research indicates that, to the contrary, there is no direct correlation between higher levels of literacy and greater job opportunities. Better indicators of economic success are race, gender, and class.

Despite the clear limits on literacy as a democratizing force, the appeal to democracy as a way of legitimizing composition studies emerged with greater force during the decade of the 1990s. As Bruce Herzberg has argued, the discourse of equal opportunity, which is very much related to the literacy myth, continues to exert immense rhetorical force. In what might be called a political turn in composition studies, arguments for the possibility of creating a better society through writing instruction have proliferated throughout the 1990s and into the new century. Many chairs of the CCCC during the 1990s used their keynote addresses as opportunities to reinforce the ideals of democracy and equal opportunity. For instance, Lester Faigley, in his 1996 address, "Literacy after the Revolution," maintained, "In a culture that is increasingly cynical about the belief that schools should offer equal opportunity to education, we have remained steadfast to the goal of literacy for equality" (41). Nell Ann Pickett, the 1997 CCCC chair, spoke of the two-year college as democracy in action (in an address of the same name). And Cynthia

Selfe, in the chair's address at the 1998 CCCC, simultaneously argued that the national project to expand computer literacy would *not* lead automatically to upward mobility and that access to computers must be extended to all students so that no one would be denied jobs because they did not have technological skills. In other words, she warned against a belief in the literacy myth—in this case, that computer literacy campaigns will lead to employment—even as she appealed to it (see 419–20).

Composition scholarship seems to be unable to write itself outside of the literacy myth. "Democracy" tends to become a slippery term—it sometimes seems to refer to a utopian vision of new society that, in Andrea Lunsford's words, values "what is 'other'": "I became a student of rhetoric and composition, though I knew only vaguely and intuitively that this field offered the conceptual, theoretical, and political ground for teaching that I was looking for—one that was radically democratic; that valued what was 'other'; . . . and that tended carefully to its effects in the world beyond as well as in the academy" (77). At other times, it seems to refer to something that already exists—American capitalist society. Sometimes democratic pedagogy appears to be aimed at empowering students to become change agents. Sometimes it seems aimed at helping them to lead middle-class lives. To get a closer look at this slippage in action, I will now turn to the work of James Berlin, whose life's work was very much dedicated to articulating a democratic pedagogy.

## BERLIN'S ARTICULATIONS OF DISCIPLINARITY AND DEMOCRACY

Berlin's final, posthumously published book, *Rhetorics, Poetics, and Cultures: Refiguring College English Studies*, represents the culmination of an effort that had begun as early as 1982, with an article published in *College English* titled "Contemporary Composition: The Major Pedagogical Theories." That effort was twofold: to establish composition studies as an intellectual discipline and to argue for the superiority of "social-epistemic" pedagogy. In fact, Berlin's opus offers one of the clearest records of the simultaneous emergence of composition studies as a discipline and of various democratic pedagogies as part and parcel of this new discipline. At the same time, as chapter 3 details, the "discipline," while still preparing managers of writing programs, was separating itself from overt attention to administration.

In the 1982 article, Berlin offers the earliest version of what would become a well-known pedagogical taxonomy.[3] He uses this taxonomy to counter what he considers a misguided notion that "the composing process is always and everywhere the same" and to argue instead that "[t]o teach writing is to argue for a version of reality" (10). His taxonomy divides pedagogical theories into four (later three) "epistemic complexes," each of which offers a distinct view of how knowledge is discovered and communicated and thus distinct "directives about invention, arrangement, and style" (10).[4] By categorizing pedagogical practices epistemologically, Berlin hopes to contribute to the disciplining of composition teachers: "Everyone teaches the process of writing, but everyone does not teach the *same* process. The test of one's competence as a composition instructor . . . resides in being able to recognize and justify the version of the process being taught, complete with all of its significance for the student" (21). As Foucault has shown, discipline also requires normalization, and part of Berlin's purpose is to promote epistemic rhetoric—which "sees the writer as a creator of meaning, a shaper of reality, rather than a passive receptor of the immutably given"—as the norm, "as the most intelligent and most practical alternative available, serving in every way the best interests of the students" (19, 10). Note here that even though Berlin argues for something different from the pedagogies of the past, he continues to argue for a norm, an approach to pedagogy that is clearly "the most intelligent" and is "serving . . . the best interests of the students." The search for the one best way, the normalizing quest, resonates with traditional systematic management aims. If the best way can be found, then it becomes essential to assure conformity from those who are teaching the course under one's direction—whether they happen to agree with that approach or not.

Already in 1982, then, Berlin had begun his dual project of establishing composition studies as an intellectual discipline and of arguing for social-epistemic rhetoric as the pedagogical standard for this discipline. At this point, Berlin's argument is based not on political convictions but on epistemological arguments. Although Berlin would come to associate social-epistemic rhetoric with Marxian versions of critical pedagogy—an association most clearly articulated in his 1988 article "Rhetoric and Ideology in the College Class"—in 1982, the word "democracy" was nowhere to be found. Instead, at a moment when cognitivist theories of pedagogy were dominant in composition studies, Berlin strategically deploys science as grounds for his claim. If most teachers use textbooks based on current-traditionalist principles, he reasons, then they are teaching an outdated worldview that arose with "the positivist view of modern science" ("Contemporary Composition" 20). But teachers know, as do "many scientists," that positivism does not address contemporary problems: "Yet most of those who use these texts would readily admit that the scientific world view has demonstrated its inability to solve the problems that most concern us. . . . And even many scientists concur with them in this view—Oppenheimer and Einstein, for example" (20). Conversely, teaching according to the epistemic principles of the New Rhetoric "will enable [students] to become effective persons as they become effective writers" (20). Berlin's concern at this point is not with the political but with the epistemological, with the way of thinking and the way of teaching that most conforms to current philosophical and scientific views. His project is establishing composition studies as a viable intellectual discipline.

A political orientation begins to emerge in Berlin's two-volume history of composition—*Writing Instruction in Nineteenth-Century American Colleges* and *Rhetoric and Reality: Writing Instruction in American Colleges, 1900–1985*. Along with this increasing politicization, these two books also continue in the double purpose of establishing the intellectual legitimacy of composition studies—this time, through setting up epistemological lineages for a diverse group of pedagogical approaches—and of arguing for the intellectual superiority of social-epistemic rhetoric. In fact, by the end of the second volume, Berlin seems to indicate that social-epistemic rhetoric has emerged as the victor in the struggle among pedagogical theories.

Berlin clearly states that one of his main purposes in writing these histories is to establish the intellectual importance of the required composition course and, by extension, the field of composition studies. In the first volume, he explains that he will be concerned with explaining "why rhetoric courses since the late nineteenth century have fallen from favor, despite the fact that they often remain among the only required courses in an otherwise elective curriculum" (*Writing Instruction* 2). Similarly, in the second volume, Berlin indicates that he is writing a history of writing instruction in order to justify the course to members of English departments:

> My reading of the rhetorical history of this period tends to vindicate the position of writing instruction in the college curriculum—particularly the freshman course, a primary concern of this study. While such vindication is superfluous to anyone knowledgeable about the history of rhetoric or the history of education—the two always having been closely related—I am aware that many in English studies are unfamiliar with this background. (*Rhetoric and Reality* 1–2)

He writes also to those involved with the teaching of composition, to assure them that they are members of an intellectual community: "I have prepared my interpretation for that large group of people who teach writing to college students—a group ranging from tenured full professors to overworked and underpaid nontenurable faculty—intending to share with them the richness of their heritage and its central place in the life of our society" (18). In writing a history of composition instruction, then, Berlin is establishing an intellectual lineage and justification for the teaching of and research about first-year writing. Note, too, that his grouping together of "tenured full professors" and "overworked and underpaid nontenurable faculty" obscures the managerial function and class process that separate them.

In addition, Berlin uses history to argue for the dominance of social-epistemic pedagogy, for treating this pedagogy as the normalizing agent in composition studies. Although he had always made his preference clear in his previous publications, it is only in the final volume of his history that Berlin is able to suggest that social-epistemic rhetoric has, in fact, emerged as dominant. At the end of *Rhetoric and Reality*, Berlin suggests that his taxonomy may not work so well to describe the current pedagogical scene because so many pedagogies are taking on epistemic characteristics. He notes a "tendency of certain rhetorics within the subjective and transactional categories to move in the direction of the epistemic, regarding rhetoric as principally a method of discovering and even creating knowledge, frequently within socially defined discourse communities," and explains: "Behind this has been what Fredric Jameson has characterized as 'the discovery of the primacy of Language or the Symbolic'" (183).

Berlin, then, is able to describe a social turn in composition studies. This social turn puts composition studies in line with what he considers to be the dominant epistemology: "Thinkers as diverse as Alfred North Whitehead, Susanne Langer, Michael Polanyi, Thomas Kuhn, Hayden White, Michel Foucault, and [Richard] Rorty have put forth the notion that the elements traditionally considered the central concerns of rhetoric—reality, interlocutor, audience, and language—are the very elements that are involved in the formation of knowledge" (*Rhetoric and Reality* 184). It is only at this moment, with the ascendency of social-epistemic rhetoric, an ascendency that Berlin clearly regards as essential for composition studies, that he extends the "social" into the "political." He concludes *Rhetoric and Reality* with one of his first explicit statements regarding the political exigencies of writing instruction: "We have begun to see that writing courses are not designed exclusively to prepare students for the workplace, although they must certainly do that. Writing courses prepare students for citizenship in a democracy, for assuming their political responsibilities, whether as leaders or simply as active participants" (188–89).

What interests me here is the convergence of the ascendency of social-epistemic rhetoric as a sign of composition studies' intellectual validity and the promotion of democratic participation as the goal of writing instruction. In other words, it is at the moment that social-epistemic rhetoric becomes the normalizing discourse in the discipline of composition studies that a political motivation emerges. It is at the moment that composition studies is articulated most closely with the hegemonic that a political discourse appears, at least in the work of Berlin. Of course, one reason for this timing is that a politicized discourse was gaining ascendency in literary studies in the late 1980s, as well, as Berlin alludes to through citing the names of such theorists as Jameson, Raymond Williams, Terry Eagleton, Edward Said, and Frank Lentricchia (198). But what seems most intriguing to me is that it is at the moment that composition studies becomes most secure as a discipline—as a necessary part of the ideological state apparatus of higher education—that it becomes most politicized, most closely identified with neo-Marxist theories.

Although Berlin draws explicitly from Marxist and poststructuralist theories in his post-1987 work, his view of a democratic society is less radical than such affiliations might suggest. In the previously cited passage, for example, he speaks of students as "assuming" certain responsibilities in society. To suggest that students will assume positions points to the ideological function of schooling, as described by Louis Althusser—to reproduce society through the interpellation of subjects. Berlin seems to accept the reproductive function of education and to assume that an acceptable version of a democratic society already exists. The function of education, in this view, is not to change society but to maintain it. And what characterizes democratic society, in Berlin's view? Berlin describes it as a postmodern marketplace of ideas: "A democracy . . . ordinarily provides political and social supports for open discussion, allowing for the free play of possibilities in the rhetorics that appear—although these possibilities are obviously never unlimited" (*Rhetoric and Reality* 5).

This notion of democracy as open debate continues in Berlin's last book, *Rhetorics, Poetics, and Cultures*. In the opening pages of this book, Berlin again appeals to history—this time, ancient Greek—to provide a justification for the discipline of composition studies and, at the same time, for his view of democracy:

> For the citizens of ancient Athens, rhetoric was at the center of education because it was at the center of political life, the deepest and most abiding concern of the city-state. The notion

that any feature of public activity could be above the concerns of politics—above the business of the polis—was unthinkable. The end of democracy, after all, was to enable open debate of all issues that impinged upon the community. (xii)

Democracy is figured here as a process that is an end in itself. Democracy *is* open debate—presumably open debate that leads to a better society.

Berlin argues in this final book that English studies—reconceived as the combination rather than the bifurcation of rhetoric (textual production) and poetic (textual interpretation)—"has a special role in the democratic educational mission" (54). He extends the argument for social-epistemic pedagogy to cover not just composition studies but all of English studies. Because language constructs reality, English classes should be devoted to the study of that process—they should focus, in other words, on cultural critique. Moreover, the classroom should function as a model of democratic practices, making open discussion a priority so that students are empowered to become actively engaged in the world outside of the classroom. Berlin regards participation as the hallmark of democratic practice:

> For democracy to function . . . , citizens must actively engage in public debate, applying reading and writing practices in the service of articulating their positions and their critiques of the positions of others. To have citizens who are unable to write and read for the public forum thus defeats the central purpose . . . of democracy . . . : to ensure that all interests are heard before a communal decision is made. (101)

Berlin's project is now thoroughly saturated with the appeal to democracy. He remains concerned with disciplinarity—now seeking to normalize not just composition studies but English studies as well. In his vision, English departments should transform themselves into training grounds for democratic citizens. However, I would argue that Berlin's view of democracy needs to be more thoroughly examined. In the next section, I will offer a context for and a critique of the limits of a disciplinary democracy.

## QUALITY MANAGEMENT AND THE
## COMMODIFICATION OF PARTICIPATION

Like most theorists of critical pedagogy, Berlin remains concerned that, even as they learn to look on society with a critical eye, students gain skills that will allow them to succeed in the workplace. At the same time, critical pedagogy has emphasized that students should not be indoctrinated in the acceptance of mindless, mechanical work. In order to avoid such indoctrination, liberatory teachers eschew what Paulo Freire has called "banking" education, in which the teacher "deposits" information in passive students (see Freire 52–67). The participatory classroom that Berlin describes is a common oppositional model: in it, students are active creators of meaning rather than passive recipients.

However, banking education is a model of education that best suits a workplace based upon rote, repetitive labor. As Berlin points out in *Rhetorics, Poetics, and Cultures*, this Fordist model of labor has been challenged by what has been called a post-Fordist model. Jobs in production are being displaced in America by jobs in service. Rather than being required to settle into assembly-line work, today's workers must be flexible. Moreover, as Berlin points out, "the managerial job market our students wish to enter values employees who are expert communicators, who are capable of performing multiple tasks, who can train quickly on the job, and who can work collaboratively with others" (46). The current job market, in other words, values the active subject that the participatory classroom seems to intend to produce. James Paul Gee, Glynda Hull, and Colin Lankshear refer to this changed workplace as "typical of the new capitalism" that focuses "on processes and reengineering of processes rather than on divisions, boundaries, and borders" (57). Berlin both acknowledges and welcomes this convergence: "We must finally provide a college education that enables workers to be excellent communicators, quick and flexible learners, and cooperative collaborators. Indeed, many of the recent changes in the English department reflect this effort" (*Rhetorics* 50). While he also argues that classrooms must do more, that they must "offer a curriculum that places preparation for work within a comprehensive range of democratic educational concerns," I would argue that "participatory" education may function as a new, postmodern version of "banking" education. To explain what I mean, I need to turn to a word that functioned in the 1990s as a commonplace in business management in much the same way that "democracy" has functioned in composition studies. That word is "quality."

"Quality" became a buzzword in management in the late 1980s and early 1990s.[5] "Total Quality Management" (TQM) and other quality initiatives arose as a response to Japanese competitiveness in the global marketplace. As TQM guru W. Edwards Deming explains, American managers have been operating under the misguided notion "that quality and productivity are incompatible: that you can not have both," whereas Japanese management recognized as early as 1948 that "improvement of quality begets naturally and inevitably improvement of productivity" (1, 2). Among the changes that an emphasis on quality brings to a corporation are increases in the responsibility of each employee and an emphasis on teamwork. Deming maintains, "People require in their careers, more than money, ever-broadening opportunities to add something to society, materially and otherwise" (86). An emphasis on producing quality (rather than simply a quantity of) products "provides . . . pride of workmanship" (1). In order to do this, workers need to know what to do and how what they do affects other people (that is, consumers). Toward this end, companies must "break down barriers between departments. People in research, design, sales, and production must work as a team, to foresee problems of production and in use that may be encountered with the product or service" (24).

Proponents of TQM regard it as a revolution in the workplace, a revolution that benefits the company and the worker.[6] And, in fact, Deming describes quality management in these terms: "Transformation of American style of management is not a job of reconstruction, nor is it revision. It requires a whole new structure, from foundation upward" (ix). However, as critics of quality management have pointed out, this transformation of the structure of management does not usually entail a transformation of the actual social relations between management and workers: "It does not necessarily extend to the enhancement of working conditions or greater control over key decisions about investment, the fundamentally hierarchical division of labour, or the organization of work" (Wilkinson and Willmott 4). Or, to use Gibson-Graham's language, TQM does not necessarily end—or even mitigate—the class process.

Although TQM purists insist that "quality" has a distinct meaning, it—like "democracy"—may be an appealing term precisely because of its "vague, but nonetheless positive, associations" (Wilkinson and Willmott 2). And like democracy, it could potentially be deployed for socially progressive ends. Sociologist Janette Webb argues, "Just as the rhetoric of equal opportunity has been used, despite its limitations, to the benefit of some groups of women, for example, so the rhetoric of TQM could conceivably be used in campaigns for more democratic management practices, improved safety systems, socially useful services and products" (124). However, Webb is not optimistic about this progressive possibility but is concerned about another: "At worst, . . . the ideology of TQM reduces honesty, integrity, authenticity . . . to marketable commodities which have a price just like any other goods; it reduces workplace relations to the 'imperatives of the marketplace' and becomes an excuse for managerial, and immoral, expediency" (125).

Given the tendency toward commodification and the subordination of all social relations to the motive for profit in late capitalist economic systems, this latter possibility for quality initiatives seems more likely than the socially transformative possibility. Similarly, it seems likely that participation and responsible citizenship, as emphasized in the "democratic" classroom, will also tend to function as marketable commodities for the quality workplace. If "'involvement,' 'participation,' 'teamwork' and the promotion of 'empowerment'" are central to the postmodern workplace, and if in our current hegemonic formation, as Chantal Mouffe suggests, "the whole set of social activities [is] . . . subordinated to the logic of production for profit," then it seems unlikely that democratic classroom practices— or quality management, for that matter—will necessarily serve to usher in a more equitable social order (Wilkinson and Willmott 13; Mouffe, "Hegemony" 92).

## FEELING DEMOCRATIC?

In addition to being susceptible to commodification, the practices that Berlin and others in composition studies identify as "democratic" tend to overlook inequities built into these practices. For example, participation—often taking the form of small group work—is highly valued as a democratic practice. However, as Evelyn Ashton-Jones and Gail Stygall have pointed out in separate articles, gender differences do not automatically go away when students work together. Ashton-Jones warns, "To remain silent on the ways that writing groups, too, can create chilly conditions for women is to perpetuate the legacy of silence that assures that these processes will continue unchecked" (22). Moreover, Jacqueline Jones Royster used her 1995 CCCC chair's address as an opportunity to question some of the enthusiasm over the field's "democratic" practices: When the speaker is marked as "other," she asked, do we really hear him or her? Do we really listen to what a person who is different from us—who, for example, is marked as a racialized other—is saying (see "When the First Voice")?

What all of these scholars are pointing to is the tendency for the subject of democracy to be conceived of as homogeneous. Simply valuing "participation" does not ensure that everyone will in fact participate on an equal basis or that everyone will be heard. As Mouffe argues, "The struggle for equality is no longer limited to the political and economic arenas. Many new rights are being defined and demanded: those of women, of homosexuals, of various regional and ethnic minorities. All inequalities existing in our society are now at issue" ("Hegemony" 100). Given this situation, democracy itself must be reconceptualized as more than simply participation in public debates:

> It is not enough to improve upon the liberal parliamentary conception of democracy by creating a number of basic democratic forums through which citizens could participate in the management of public affairs, or workers in the management of industries. In addition to these traditional social subjects [that is, citizens and workers] we must recognize the existence of others

and their political characters: women and the various minorities also have a right to equality and to self-determination. (100)

Mouffe maintains that "we must institutionalize a true pluralism, a *pluralism of subjects*," in which "we transcend a certain individualistic notion of rights and . . . elaborate a central notion of *solidarity*" (100). What Mouffe calls for is nothing short of a new hegemonic regime, "a new symbolic ordering of social relations," a new definition of what constitutes the common good ("Rethinking" 176; see also 179). In Mouffe's view, a radically democratic society is something to be struggled for; it is not something that exists. She contends that "the problem with liberal democratic societies—*really existing* liberal democracies—is not their ideals; their ideals are wonderful. The problem is that those ideals are not put into practice in those societies. So the question that I think radical democracy is very much about is how to force those societies to take those ideals seriously, to put them into practice" (196).

What's curious about Mouffe's language here, however, is the word "force." Can people in societies be "forced" to do even those things that many of us might regard as essential to justice? We know, in the wake of such tragedies as the wars in Vietnam and Iraq, that democracy itself cannot be forced. Following upon Jon Beasley-Murray's explication of the Spanish *Requirimento*, recounted in chapter 2, we can see that the very "articulation" or speaking forth of "choice" may itself function as a way to inculcate a feeling of rightness in those who are speaking it. It may not, in fact, offer a real choice.

Argument—the expression of positions and reasons—has been the traditional basis of democratic process. As a result, the teaching of rhetoric, as in Berlin, has seemed to be the foundation of ensuring the continuation of democracy. Perhaps, however, this articulation between "democracy" and "rational argument" is part of the problem. Sharon Crowley, in her recent *Toward a Civil Discourse*, makes a similar claim about the failure of liberal notions of rationality to affect change at the level of belief. "While people do reason by connecting factual evidence to premises," she writes, "premises are themselves drawn from ideologies or from systems of belief that are even more resistant to change, such as metaphysics, theology, or hegemonic discourses. . . . Images can stimulate visceral responses, which can in turn reinforce belief" (100–101). "Visceral responses," she notes, are connected to affect, and it is the full rhetorical repertoire, including appeals to ethos and pathos, that must be harnessed in order to effect change at the level of beliefs and values: "Cicero suggests . . . that rhetorical effect is achieved by means of affect: the beliefs and behaviors of audiences are altered not only by the provision of proofs but by establishment of ethical, evaluating, and emotional climates in which such changes can occur" (58). The language of "climates" here resonates with Jenny Edbauer's theory of "rhetorical ecologies." For Edbauer, rhetorical affect isn't simply a static proof but manifests through the circulation of affect. Yet for Edbauer, affect is not so easily controlled: once deployed, rhetorical discourse freely circulates and may be redeployed in new contexts, affecting people in new ways. In other words, from my reading of Edbauer, affect is not so much a rhetorical "tool" as a difficult to control, often aconscious dimension of rhetoric.

We may be able to contribute to a climate, then, but a contained argument, whether "rational" or affect-laden, is unlikely to effect change. Change happens as affect circulates, and so democracies, which are simply groups of people agreeing to make decisions together and equally, may indeed be held together or morph through space and time by way of circulation.

What might this mean, then, for "democratic" pedagogies? First, the very fact that these pedagogies, these ways of believing, have indeed circulated widely in the field of composition studies suggests that they have had an effect: the dominance of politically based pedagogies in the 1990s and into the twenty-first century implies a tendency among composition scholars to *feel the rightness* of such pedagogies. But because pedagogies also always circulate as managerial tools deployed by writing program administrators, they also function, through their repetition, to seemingly persuade composition teachers of their rightness. Given how difficult it can sometimes be to assimilate a new pedagogy, however, and given that different teachers may come to programs with different habitual *feelings* about the teaching of writing, tension between the expectations of administration and the performance of teachers is almost inevitable. In such cases, the felt importance of political pedagogies may result in feelings of guilt or performances of what is often labeled "resistance" among teachers (see Drew et al. and Crawford and Strickland for a discussion of guilt; Ebest for extended discussion of resistance).

Methods of cultivating "democratic" workplaces and classrooms through the teaching of argument and the cultivation of collaboration are not "bad"; they are simply limited. If we accept that limitation, what does that mean for the future of democratic, progressive pedagogies and democratic, progressive workplaces? Is it possible to enact not simply different social arrangements (like more discussion among groups) but also a different economic model, a different class process? I'll offer one brief possibility in the afterword.

## Afterword: Tweaking It—Toward Operative Managerial Reason in Composition Studies

THIS BOOK HAS NOT ASPIRED toward totality, has not hoped to have the final word on composition studies and the role of management in the field. Rather, it has been an effort to understand the field as fundamentally managerial, to see the managerial as an imperative energizing the field throughout its history. This energy has been productive, leading the way to professional organizations, to innovative scholarship, to new ways of practicing teaching, writing, and, yes, administration.

Even so, the managerial unconscious, the marginalizing and even denying of the necessary managerial function of administrative work, has obscured the default class function that administration plays in a stratified society, in stratified workplaces, and in stratified university programs. This unconscious, I hope I've made clear, comes from an affective association that prefers teaching and that is averse to the pejorative connotations of management in a humanistic and occasionally Marxist field of study. But to avoid the managerial because of its associations with a disparaged capitalistic or mechanistic workplace is to fall into what J. K. Gibson-Graham call a kind of "capitalocentrism," a belief that capitalism is the only economic system, that any kind of management is always already corrupted.

To deny the managerial is simply, by default, to practice the dominant sort of management, which is based on a control that seeks to change the affective stances of workers in order to secure the benefits of their surplus labor. What difference might it make, then, to understand the managerial as already operative in the work we do as administrators and as composition scholars? To consider ways in which it might operate as something other than a class function or mechanistic control? Two possibilities come to mind, one concrete and one theoretical. I'll begin with the concrete.

I mentioned in the introduction to this book that I worked as a coordinator of the first-semester composition course at my doctoral institution while working toward my degree in rhetoric and composition. As part of this position, I had the rather extraordinary opportunity not simply to help design curricula and supervise teachers implementing those curricula but also to join with a group of critically minded administrators (three other graduate/non-tenuretrack administrators and our tenured leader) dedicated to scrutinizing our work as administrators. Our leader invited us to reflect with her on the assumptions and emotional allegiances we brought to writing program administration. As Alice Gillam, our tenured administrator, relates in "Collaboration, Ethics, and the Emotional Labor of WPAs," we thought together about the difference our various statuses made in our approach to managing the program, the ways in which our status as graduate students sometimes made it easier for us to not *feel* invested in maintaining the program in the way that she did, that we didn't see it as some sort of failure if the program were to fundamentally change, to move away from some of its normalizing commitments (see also Crawford and Strickland). We engaged also in some difficult conversations about the way that the large-scale portfolio assessment system that had been in place for a decade or more potentially took autonomy away from teachers, even as norming sessions sought to make them *feel* that the system was objective and fair. The combination of Alice's openness and our own lack of division as graduate students—we hadn't yet put into operation the managerial unconscious, the splitting off of our cultural-critical abilities from our administrative work—meant that we were able to hold these talks and to put them into practice, to begin to *tweak* the portfolio system, to experiment with more context-rich, small-scale portfolio assessment, one that left room for plenty of teacherly autonomy.

And "tweaking" is ultimately the action that what I want to call an *operative* approach to management offers. An operative approach to management leaves nothing off the table—it calls us to notice and investigate our emotional stances toward our work, our beliefs about what constitutes a successful program, our beliefs even about the very values we see in the teaching of writing and about what we think makes a good teacher of writing. And this investigation may open up dissatisfaction—perhaps even the kind of disappointment that Laura Micciche, another of my graduate administrative collaborators, describes in her important essay "More Than a Feeling: Disappointment and WPA Work." But this dissatisfaction can catalyze action, is indeed the forerunner to action.

I take the term "operative reason" from communication theorist Brian Massumi. For Massumi, operative reason "is the experimental crafting . . . of the practically impossible" (111). It is a kind of *intuiting* into what might work differently. It is, Massumi continues, "a process of trial and error, with occasional shots in the dark, guided in every case by a pragmatic sense of the situation's responsivity (as opposed to its manipulability)" (112). Operative reason is distinguished from the more familiar instrumental reason in that it "poses an unpredictable futurity rather than anticipating outcomes" (110).

No anticipating outcomes? Is this still writing program administration? It isn't that outcomes are "bad." As Massumi is fond of saying, "It is not a question of right or wrong—nothing important ever is" (13). Rather, recognizing that composition professionals *do* management, we can put our considerable intellectual abilities to work on the pragmatic, transformative tasks of tweaking, of deploying our work as "*performances* requiring audience participation" (97). That's what I understand my writing program administration leader to have been doing in inviting us to perform administrative work with her—working together to pose unpredictable futurities.

As people with "a foot in both camps" of the discipline of rhetoric and composition and the administration of writing programs, as Joseph Harris puts it (see "Thinking Like a Program"), can we ask questions that go beyond the instrumental questions of how to "get things done" to include questions of the ethical and political consequences of doing so? Can we put to question the most basic assumptions that we hold—that teaching is a fundamental good, that writing is a fundamental necessity, that "good writing" is something we know how to describe? Certainly, such scholars as Alice Gillam, Jeanne Gunner, Laura Micciche, Eileen Schell, and Harris himself have begun to ask such questions in their work. The collection that Gunner and I recently edited also functions as a site for such critical inquiry. But we can do much more. We can embrace the role of manager, not because it is a good or because it is the only way to get things done. We can embrace it because it is ours and because it deserves much more attention if we are to truly work for the material benefit of administrators, teachers, and students alike.

NOTES
WORKS CITED
INDEX

### Introduction: Composition Studies' Managerial Unconscious

1. Full disclosure: My own chapter, "The Managerial Unconscious of Composition Studies," a precursor of this book, appeared in that collection and is also cited in Bousquet's *minnesota review* article.

2. I am indebted to Hardin's "The Writing Program Administrator and Enlightened False Consciousness: The Virtues of Becoming an Empty Signifier," which first prompted me to think of writing program administration as function rather than identity.

3. Bringing this kind of critical scrutiny to the work of writing program administration is the goal of the collection that I have coedited with Jeanne Gunner, *The Writing Program Interrupted: Making Space for Critical Discourse.*

### 1. The Emergence of Writing Programs and the Cultural Work of Composition Teaching

1. This advertisement is reproduced in Yates (44).

2. I use the term "secretarial work" to refer to all office work involving the transcription of words. In actual divisions of office labor, however, secretaries, who usually report to only one person, are of a higher rank than typists and stenographers, who generally are part of a clerical "pool." See Davies and Strom.

3. Foucault's analysis of the "means of correct training" in *Discipline and Punish* offers a yet more detailed examination of the managed body as the body writing and written.

4. For a compelling history of the influence of scientific management on American public schools, see Callahan.

5. The expectation that teachers of children should stick to monotonous drill is similar to the advice given to mothers in the early decades of the twentieth century. As Ehrenreich and English explain, "The goal was industrial man—disciplined, efficient, precise—whether it was his lot to

be an industrial laborer, a corporate leader, or another expert himself. The key to producing such a man was *regularity*" (181).

6. The wide circulation of the figure of the nurturing teacher in contemporary pedagogical theory represents, I would argue, an effort to dissociate the woman teacher from the image of the old-maid grammarian in order to realign her with the cultural expectations of womanhood. As Worsham suggests, "Women teachers always labor under the obligation to provide the (maternal) breast. Nurturance, in other words, is an obligation for women who live and labor in an economy that recognizes them only as providers of an all too often sexualized nurturance" (242; see also Schell, "Cost of Caring" 74–81). In another instance of simultaneous emergence, the resexualization of the woman teacher through the discourse of nurturance parallels the sexualization of the secretary in popular culture. (For a critique of representations of secretaries, see Pringle.)

7. I am indebted to Sandra Jones, who has discussed the tendency of white people to assert ownership over standard English, for this formulation.

## 2. Teaching Subjects: Professionalism and the Discourse of Disorder

1. This claim, however, *is* suggested by Deleuze, and in turn by Hardt and Negri, who understand Empire to be one with administered society or "control society."

2. The communications course, which brought together speaking and writing, was a popular alternative to the composition course. It was, however, short-lived; by 1962, Kitzhaber reported that few communications courses were still being taught (*Themes*). Essentially, the communications course had the same function as the composition course: it was a required first-year course that was intended to introduce students to language practices appropriate to the university. For a more nuanced history of this class, see George and Trimbur.

3. Nystrand and his colleagues place the date even later, with the development in the 1970s of journals devoted to composition research. As I will argue in the next chapter, the 1970s do in fact mark a significant moment in the formation of composition studies as a discipline.

4. Gorelik, for example, argues that the effort to professionalize schoolteachers in the late nineteenth and early twentieth centuries represented an effort to exert control over teachers without a concomitant economic benefit to the teachers.

5. See Crowley, "Composition's Ethic of Service," for a critique of the discourse of student needs.

6. The workshop participants did conclude, however, that the "the problem of financial status was felt to underlie all other questions of

status" ("Professional" 12). While they acknowledged that the "composition teacher suffers from having no organization, no union, to protect him," they did not consider it to be within the scope of the CCCC to attend to this economic problem (12).

7. Harris identifies the "genre of what-those-damn-teachers-do-to-kids stories" with the advent of process pedagogy (*Teaching Subject* 62). I would agree with this linkage, and I see both the pedagogy and the trope as symptomatic of a larger movement—the movement to intervene in and control the behavior of the teacher.

8. As Harris points out, Emig also tends to describe the kind of writing and teaching she is opposed to in mechanistic terms (*Teaching Subject* 60–61).

## 3. You Say You Want a Revolution? Managed Universities, Managerial Affects

1. Among the histories that have helped to reify the idea of a "current-traditional rhetoric" are those by Berlin and Crowley. This reification has been challenged by Paine's archival history of two so-called current-traditionalists, *The Resistant Writer*.

2. According to Drucker, the boomlet of enthusiastic books on management in the late 1960s was simultaneously a sign of the general public's saturation with management and a sure harbinger of management's decline. He first establishes that "[b]y the late sixties American publishers alone brought out each year several hundred management titles—four or five times as many in one year as there had been written altogether in all the years before World War II," adding in a footnote that "management books have achieved the impossible: they have become best sellers—e.g., Alfred P. Sloan Jr.'s *My Years with General Motors*" (14).

3. The literature on the "corporate," "managed," or "entrepreneurial" university is vast. An excellent place to begin is with Slaughter and Leslie's *Academic Capitalism*, which traces the economic shifts globally that have effected changes in universities in North America and beyond. Aronowitz's *Knowledge Factory* makes a direct connection between Kerr's "multiversity" and the corporate university. Newfield's *Ivy and Industry* traces the connection between universities, including the humanities, and managerial discourse back to the nineteenth century. Bousquet's *How the University Works* considers the effects of the corporate university on student and faculty labor. Other significant studies include Donoghue and Rhoades, among others.

4. In the 1950s and especially the 1960s, there was a shifting between references to the "freshman course" and references to the "freshman program." In other words, the idea of a program seems to have been a postwar

phenomenon, making references to programs before 1950 somewhat anachronistic. The idea of a "program" appears to have gained strength with the multiversity and, especially, with the influx of basic writing "programs" (not just courses).

5. The connection between the founding of the WPA and the growing significance of basic writing *programs* can be deduced in part from the connection between the WPA and a precursor formed at CUNY, the center of open admissions. As recounted by Kenneth Bruffee, the first meeting of what would become the WPA was at the MLA convention in 1976: "Harvey Weiner started CAWS [CUNY Association of Writing Supervisors], the precursor to WPA . . . [that] brought people together out of the woodwork. . . . [WPA began] at MLA in Chicago in 1976 . . . , and Ed Corbett was elected to head it up, but he didn't want to do it, so I did it. . . . Harvey and I conspired to set up WPA" (qtd. in Heckathorn 216).

6. The ten suggested names were as follows: Council on College Rhetoric, Council on English Composition, Council on College Composition, Council on College Communications, Council on College Writing, College Communications Council, Conference on College Composition, College Writing Council, Council on Freshman English, College Writing Association (as reported by Bird).

7. A striking anecdote that speaks to the fiscal crisis comes from a 1976 letter written by Richard Larson to NCTE:

> Lehman was closed two weeks in June, along with the rest of CUNY, for want of operating funds. Then the Legislature gave us money to get through the academic year, and gave us a budget for next year that required heavy cuts at all the colleges. . . . About a hundred and fifty people, including ninety or so faculty, had to be fired, and we had to check to determine whom we could fire, then write letters of termination.

8. In an interesting and instructive parallel/reversal, Drucker holds that the work of a manager is more like a teacher than like most other professions:

> Unlike the work of the physician, the stonemason or the lawyer, management must always be done in an organization—that is, within a web of human relations. The manager, therefore, is always an example. What he does is important. But equally important is who he is—far more important than it is with respect to the physician, stonemason or even lawyer. Only the teacher has the same twofold dimension, the dimension of skill and performance, and the dimension of personality, example and integrity. (xii)

## 4. Democratic Pedagogies and the Persistence of Control

1. Miller, Brueggemann, Blue, and Shepherd find in their national survey of rhetoric and composition graduate students that many have become disillusioned and no longer expect to find a tenure-track job. The researchers suggest that their disillusionment is not misguided; the market has become relatively glutted with composition specialists. While there are, no doubt, a greater number of students competing for tenure-track jobs in composition than even ten years ago, a person with training in composition continues to have greater job prospects than a person with training in a literary field.

2. As Olson notes, "Progressivist criticism has . . . become central to much of the work we do today. Many of the notions of such theorists as Freire, Ohmann, and Sledd that seemed so shockingly revolutionary in the 1970s now regularly inform composition scholarship, and even official NCTE and CCCC resolutions" (297).

3. Berlin offered his taxonomy in response to other scholars' taxonomies; he cites the work of Richard Fulkerson, David V. Harrington, and William F. Woods as "articles attempting to make sense of the various approaches to teaching composition" ("Contemporary Composition" 9). Certainly, the effort to "make sense" of and systematize knowledge about composition indicates a movement toward disciplinarity.

4. In 1982, these four groups were the Neo-Aristotelians (Classicists), the Positivists (Current-Traditionalists), the Neo-Platonists (Expressionists), and the New Rhetoricians (Epistemics). The Classicists were subsumed under the last category in the more familiar tripartite division that Berlin described in *Rhetoric and Reality*: objective theories (including current-traditional and behavioral pedagogies), subjective theories (including belletristic and expressionist pedagogies), and transactional theories (including classical, cognitive, and epistemic pedagogies).

5. One sign of the ubiquity of "quality" in the late twentieth century is in the name change of a major in the School of Business at my doctoral-granting institution, the University of Wisconsin–Milwaukee: "Production and Operations Management" became "Quality Production and Operations Management" in the mid-1990s.

6. See Rhodes for an application of TQM to writing program administration.

# WORKS CITED

Adams, Charles Francis, Edwin Lawrence Godkin, and George R. Nutter. *Report of the Committee on Composition and Rhetoric.* 1897. Brereton, *Origins* 101–27.

Adams, Charles Francis, Edwin Lawrence Godkin, and Josiah Quincy. *Report of the Committee on Composition and Rhetoric.* 1892. Brereton, *Origins* 73–100.

Adler-Kassner, Linda. *The Activist WPA: Changing Stories about Writing and Writers.* Logan: Utah State UP, 2008.

"Administration of the Composition Course." *CCC* 1.2 (May 1950): 40–42.

Amott, Teresa, and Julie Matthaei. *Race, Gender, and Work: A Multicultural Economic History of Women in the United States.* Rev. ed. Boston: South End, 1996.

Aronowitz, Stanley. *The Knowledge Factory: Dismantling the Corporate University and Creating True Higher Learning.* Boston: Beacon, 2001.

"Articulating High School and College Work: The Report of Workshop No. 12." *CCC* 1.2 (May 1950): 37–39.

Ashton-Jones, Evelyn. "Collaboration, Conversation, and the Politics of Gender." *Feminine Principles and Women's Experience in American Composition and Rhetoric.* Ed. Louise Wetherbee Phelps and Janet Emig. Pittsburgh: U of Pittsburgh P, 1995. 5–26.

Banks, Will, and Jonathan Alexander. "Queer Eye for the Comp Program: Toward a Queer Critique of WPA Work." Strickland and Gunner 86–98.

Bataille, Robert R. "Hiring Composition Specialists." *WPA: Writing Program Administration* 4.1 (1980): 17–22.

Beasley-Murray, Jon. *Posthegemony: Political Theory and Latin America.* Minneapolis: U of Minnesota P, 2010.

Bederman, Gail. *Manliness and Civilization: A Cultural History of Gender and Race in the United States, 1880–1917.* Chicago: U of Chicago P, 1996.

Berlin, James A. "Contemporary Composition: The Major Pedagogical Theories." *College English* 44 (1982): 765–77. Rpt. in *The Writing*

*Teacher's Sourcebook*. Ed. Gary Tate, Edward P. J. Corbett, and Nancy Myers. 3rd ed. New York: Oxford UP, 1994. 9–21.

———. "Rhetoric and Ideology in the Writing Class." *College English* 50 (1988): 477–94.

———. *Rhetoric and Reality: Writing Instruction in American Colleges, 1900–1985*. Carbondale: Southern Illinois UP, 1987.

———. *Rhetorics, Poetics, and Cultures: Refiguring College English Studies*. Urbana, IL: NCTE, 1996.

———. *Writing Instruction in Nineteenth-Century American Colleges*. Carbondale: Southern Illinois UP, 1984.

Bérubé, Michael. *The Employment of English*. New York: New York UP, 1998.

Bird, Nancy K. "The Conference on College Composition and Communication: A Historical Study of Its Continuing Education and Professional Activities, 1949–1975." Diss. Virginia Polytechnic Institute and State University, 1977.

Birnbaum, Robert. *Management Fads in Higher Education: Where They Come From, What They Do, Why They Fail*. San Francisco: Jossey-Bass, 2001.

Bledstein, Burton J. *The Culture of Professionalism: The Middle Class and the Development of Higher Education in America*. New York: Norton, 1976.

Bousquet, Marc. *How the University Works: Higher Education and the Low-Wage Nation*. New York: New York UP, 2008.

———. "The Rhetoric of 'Job Market' and the Reality of the Labor System." *College English* 66 (2003): 207–28.

———. "Tenured Bosses and Disposable Teachers." *minnesota review* n.s. 58–60 (2003). Web. 4 Aug. 2009. <http://www.theminnesotareview. org/journal/ns58/bousquet.htm>.

Bousquet, Marc, Tony Scott, and Leo Parascondola, eds. *Tenured Bosses and Disposable Teachers: Writing Instruction in the Managed University*. Carbondale: Southern Illinois UP, 2004.

Bové, Paul. *In the Wake of Theory*. Middletown, CT: Wesleyan UP, 1992.

Braverman, Harry. *Labor and Monopoly Capital: The Degradation of Work in the Twentieth Century*. 1974. Anniversary ed. New York: Monthly Review, 1998.

Brereton, John C. Introduction. Brereton, *Origins* 3–25.

———, ed. *The Origins of Composition Studies in American Colleges, 1875–1925: A Documentary History*. Pittsburgh: U of Pittsburgh P, 1995.

Briggs, LeBaron Russell. "The Harvard Admission Examination in English." 1888. Brereton, *Origins* 57–73.

Brody, Miriam. *Manly Writing: Gender, Rhetoric, and the Rise of Composition*. Carbondale: Southern Illinois UP, 1993.

Brown, Stuart, Rebecca Jackson, and Theresa Enos. "The Arrival of Rhetoric in the Twenty-First Century: The 1999 Survey of Doctoral Programs in Rhetoric." *Rhetoric Review* 18 (2000): 233–42.

Brown, Stuart, Paul Meyer, and Theresa Enos. "Doctoral Programs in Rhetoric and Composition." *Rhetoric Review* 12 (1994): 240-51.

Brown, Walter Rollo. *Dean Briggs.* 1926. Brereton, *Origins* 28–33.

Bruffee, Kenneth. "Editorial." *WPA: Writing Program Administration* 1.3 (1978a): 6–12.

———. "Editorial." WPA: Writing Program Administration 2.3 (1978b): 3.

———. "Editorial." WPA: Writing Program Administration 3.1 (1979): 7–8.

———. "Editorial." WPA: Writing Program Administration 4.1 (1980): 7–9.

———. "Editorial." WPA: Writing Program Administration 7.1–2 (1983): 11–12.

Bryan, Adolphus J. "The Problem of Freshman English in the University." *CCC* 2.2 (May 1951): 6–8.

Bullock, Richard H., and John Trimbur, eds. *The Politics of Writing Instruction: Postsecondary.* Portsmouth, NH: Boynton/Cook, 1991.

Callahan, Raymond E. *Education and the Cult of Efficiency.* Chicago: U of Chicago P, 1962.

Campbell, Oscar James. "The Failure of Freshman English." *English Journal* (College Edition) 28 (1939): 177–85.

Carnegie Commission on Higher Education. *Opportunities for Women in Higher Education.* New York: McGraw-Hill, 1973.

CCCC Preliminary Program, 1970. NCTE Archives. Urbana, IL.

Chandler, Alfred D. *The Visible Hand: The Managerial Revolution in American Business.* Cambridge: Belknap/Harvard UP, 1977.

"The Chicago Convention." *College English* 10.5 (Feb. 1949): 283–88.

Classifieds. *Indianapolis Star* 12 Mar. 2000: F1–F20.

Connors, Robert J. *Composition-Rhetoric: Backgrounds, Theory, and Pedagogy.* Pittsburgh: U of Pittsburgh P, 1997.

———. "Mechanical Correctness as a Focus in Composition Instruction." CCC 36 (1985): 61–72.

———. "Rhetoric in the Modern University: The Creation of an Underclass." Bullock and Trimbur 55–84.

"Constitution and By-Laws of the Conference on College Composition and Communication." *CCC* 3.3 (Oct. 1952): 19–24.

Corbett, Edward P. J. "A History of Writing Program Administration." *Learning from the Histories of Rhetoric: Essays in Honor of Winifred Bryan Horner.* Ed. Theresa Enos. Carbondale: Southern Illinois UP, 1993. 60–73.

Council of Writing Program Administrators. "Evaluating the Intellectual Work of Writing Program Administrators." Council of Writing Program Administrators, 1998. Web. 4 Aug. 2009. <http://wpacouncil.org/positions/intellectualwork.html>.

Crawford, Ilene Whitney, and Donna Strickland. "Interrupting Collaboration: Feminist Writing Program Administration and the Question of Status." *Performing Feminism and Administration in Rhetoric and Composition Studies.* Ed. Krista Ratcliffe and Becky Rickly. Cresskill, NJ: Hampton, 2010. 77–91.

Critical Management Studies Division. Domain Statement. Academy of Management, 2010. Web. 23 Feb. 2011. <http://group.aomonline.org/cms/About/domain.htm>.

Crowley, Sharon. *Composition in the University: Historical and Polemical Essays.* Pittsburgh: U of Pittsburgh P, 1998.

———. "Composition's Ethic of Service, the Universal Requirement, and the Discourse of Student Need." *JAC: A Journal of Composition Theory* 15 (1995): 227–39.

———. "Early Concerns of CCCC." Conference on College Composition and Communication Convention. Palmer House, Chicago. 2 Apr. 1998.

———. *Toward a Civil Discourse: Rhetoric and Fundamentalism.* Pittsburgh: U of Pittsburgh P, 2006.

Daumer, Elizabeth, and Sandra Runzo. "Transforming the Composition Classroom." *Teaching Writing: Pedagogy, Gender, and Equity.* Ed. Cynthia L. Caywood and Gillian R. Overing. Albany: State U of New York P, 1987. 45–62.

Davies, Margery W. *Woman's Place Is at the Typewriter: Office Work and Office Workers, 1870–1930.* Philadelphia: Temple UP, 1982.

Deleuze, Gilles. "Postscript on Control Societies." *Negotiations 1972–1990.* Tr. Martin Joughin. New York: Columbia UP, 1995.

Deming, W. Edwards. *Out of the Crisis.* Cambridge: MIT P, 1982.

"Doctoral Programs in Rhetoric and Composition." *Rhetoric Review* 18 (2000): 244–373.

Donoghue, Frank. *The Last Professors: The Corporate University and the Fate of the Humanities.* New York: Fordham UP, 2008.

Drew, Chris, et al. "Affect, Labor, and the Graduate Teaching Assistant: Can Writing Programs Become 'Spaces of Hope'?" *Works and Days* 21 (2003): 169–86.

Drucker, Peter F. *Management: Tasks, Responsibilities, Practices.* 1973. HarperBusiness ed. Abridged and revised. New York: Harper Collins, 1993.

Dykema, Karl W. "The Problem of Freshman English in the Liberal Arts College." *CCC* 2.2 (May 1951): 3–5.

Ebest, Sally Barr. *Changing the Way We Teach: Writing and Resistance in the Training of Teaching Assistants.* Carbondale: Southern Illinois UP, 2005.

Edbauer, Jenny. "Unframing Models of Public Distribution: From Rhetorical Situations to Rhetorical Ecologies." *Rhetoric Society Quarterly* 35 (2005): 5–24.

Ehrenreich, Barbara, and John Ehrenreich. "The Professional-Managerial Class." *Radical America*, part 1, 11 (Mar.–Apr. 1977): 7–31; part 2, 11 (May–June 1977): 7–22. Rpt. in *Between Labor and Capital: The Professional-Managerial Class.* Ed. Pat Walker. Boston: South End, 1979.

Ehrenreich, Barbara, and Deirdre English. *For Her Own Good: 150 Years of the Experts' Advice to Women.* Garden City, NY: Anchor/Doubleday, 1978.

Elbow, Peter. *Writing Without Teachers.* New York: Oxford, 1973.

Eliot, Charles William. *Educational Reform.* New York: Century, 1909.

Emig, Janet. *The Composing Processes of Twelfth Graders.* Urbana, IL: NCTE, 1971.

Enos, Theresa. *Gender Roles and Faculty Lives in Rhetoric and Composition.* Carbondale: Southern Illinois UP, 1996.

Faigley, Lester. "Literacy after the Revolution." *CCC* 48 (1997): 30–43.

Flannery, Kathryn T. *The Emperor's New Clothes: Literature, Literacy, and the Ideology of Style.* Pittsburgh: U of Pittsburgh P, 1995.

Foucault, Michel. *Discipline and Punish: The Birth of the Prison.* Trans. Alan Sheridan. New York: Vintage/Random House, 1979.

———. "Nietzsche, Genealogy, History." *Language, Counter-memory, Practice.* Ed. Donald F. Bouchard. Ithaca: Cornell UP, 1977. 139–64.

Freire, Paulo. *Pedagogy of the Oppressed.* 1973. New York: Continuum, 1993.

Fulkerson, Richard. "Four Philosophies of Composition." *CCC* 30 (1979): 343–48.

Gee, James Paul, Glynda Hull, and Colin Lankshear. *The New Work Order: Behind the Language of the New Capitalism.* Boulder, CO: Westview, 1996.

George, Diana, ed. *Kitchen Cooks, Plate Twirlers and Troubadours: Writing Program Administrators Tell Their Stories.* Portsmouth, NH: Boynton/Cook-Heinemann, 1999.

George, Diana, and John Trimbur. "The 'Communication Battle,' or Whatever Happened to the 4th C?" *CCC* 50 (1999): 682–98.

Gerber, John. "The Conference on College Composition and Communication." *CCC* 1.1 (Mar. 1950): 12.

Gibson-Graham, J. K. *The End of Capitalism (as We Knew It): A Feminist Critique of Political Economy.* Oxford: Blackwell, 1996.

Gillam, Alice. "Collaboration, Ethics, and the Emotional Labor of WPAs." *A Way to Move: Rhetorics of Emotion and Composition Studies.* Ed. Dale Jacobs and Laura R. Micciche. Portsmouth, NH: Boynton/Cook, 2003. 113–23.

Gorelik, Sherry. "Class Relations and the Development of the Teaching Profession." *Class and Social Development: A New Theory of the Middle Class.* Ed. Dale L. Johnson. Beverly Hills: Sage, 1982. 203–23.

Graff, Harvey. *The Literacy Myth: Cultural Integration and Social Structure in the Nineteenth Century.* New York: Academic, 1979.

Gramsci, Antonio. *Selections from the Prison Notebooks of Antonio Gramsci.* Trans. and ed. Quintin Hoare and Geoffrey Nowell Smith. New York: International, 1971.

Gunner, Jeanne. "Doomed to Repeat It? A Needed Space for Critique in Historical Recovery." L'Eplattenier and Mastrangelo 263–78.

Halloran, S. Michael. "From Rhetoric to Composition: The Teaching of Writing in America to 1900." *A Short History of Writing Instruction from Ancient Greece to Twentieth-Century America.* Ed. James J. Murphy. Davis, CA: Hermagoras, 1990. 151–82.

Hardin, Joe Marshall. "The Writing Program Administrator and Enlightened False Consciousness: The Virtues of Becoming an Empty Signifier." Strickland and Gunner 137–46.

Hardt, Michael, and Antonio Negri. *Empire.* Cambridge, MA: Harvard UP, 2000.

Hariman, Robert. "The Rhetoric of Inquiry and the Professional Scholar." *Rhetoric in the Human Sciences.* Ed. Herbert W. Simons. Newbury Park, CA: Sage, 1989. 211–31.

Harris, Joseph. *A Teaching Subject: Composition since 1966.* Upper Saddle River, NJ: Prentice Hall, 1997.

———. "Thinking Like a Program." *Pedagogy* 4 (2004): 357–63.

Heckathorn, Amy. "Moving Toward a Group Identity: WPA Professionalization from the 1940s to the 1970s." L'Eplattenier and Mastrangelo 191–219.

Herbst, Jurgen. *And Sadly Teach: Teacher Education and Professionalization in American Culture.* Madison: U of Wisconsin P, 1991.

Herzberg Bruce. "Composition and the Politics of the Curriculum." *The Politics of Writing Instruction: Postsecondary.* Ed. Richard Bullock and John Trimbur. Portsmouth, NH: Boynton, 1991. 97–118.

Hill, Adams Sherman. "An Answer to the Cry for More English." 1879. Brereton, *Origins* 45–57.

Hoare, Quintin, and Geoffrey Nowell Smith. Preface. *Selections from the Prison Notebooks of Antonio Gramsci.* By Antonio Gramsci. New York: International, 1971.

Holbrook, Sue Ellen. "Women's Work: the Feminizing of Composition." *Rhetoric Review* 9 (1991): 201–29.

Horner, Bruce. "Discoursing Basic Writing." *CCC* 47 (1996): 199–222.

―――. *Terms of Work for Composition: A Materialist Critique.* Albany: State U of New York P, 2000.

Jameson, Fredric. "Cognitive Mapping." *Marxism and the Interpretation of Culture.* Ed. Cary Nelson and Lawrence Grossberg. Urbana: U of Illinois P, 1988. 347–57.

―――. *Postmodernism, or, The Cultural Logic of Late Capitalism.* Durham, NC: Duke UP, 1991.

Janangelo, Joseph, and Kristine Hansen. *Resituating Writing: Constructing and Administering Writing Programs.* Portsmouth, NH: Heinemann-Boynton/Cook, 1995.

Jarratt, Susan C., and Lynn Worsham, eds. *Feminism and Composition Studies: In Other Words.* New York: MLA, 1998.

Jewell, Walter. "The Contribution of Administrative Leadership to Academic Excellence." *WPA: Writing Program Administration* 3.3 (1980): 9–13.

Jones, Jacqueline. *American Work: Four Centuries of Black and White Labor.* New York: Norton, 1998.

Jones, Sandra E. "The Racism Within: Exorcizing Whiteness from Standard English." CCCC Convention. Palmer House, Chicago. 4 Apr. 1998.

Kerr, Clark. *The Uses of the University.* Cambridge, MA: Harvard UP, 1963.

Kitzhaber, Albert R. *Rhetoric in American Colleges, 1850–1900.* 1953. Dallas: Southern Methodist UP, 1990.

―――. Themes, Theories, and Therapy: Teaching of Writing in College. New York: McGraw-Hill, 1963.

Laclau, Ernesto, and Chantal Mouffe. *Hegemony and Socialist Strategy: Towards a Radical Democratic Politics.* New York: Verso, 1985.

Larson, Richard L. Letter to Nancy Prichard, NCTE, 1976. NCTE Archives. Urbana, IL.

L'Eplattenier, Barbara, and Lisa Mastrangelo, eds. *Historical Studies of Writing Program Administration: Individuals, Communities, and the Formation of a Discipline.* West Lafayette, IN: Parlor, 2004.

Logan, Shirley Wilson. *"We Are Coming": The Persuasive Discourse of Nineteenth-Century Black Women.* Carbondale: Southern Illinois UP, 1999.

―――. "'When and Where I Enter': Race, Gender, and Composition Studies." Jarratt and Worsham 45–57.

Lonn, Ella. "Academic Status of Women on University Faculties." *Journal of the American Association of University Women* 17 (Jan.–Mar. 1924): 5–11.

Lukács, Georg. *History and Class Consciousness: Studies in Marxist Dialectics.* Trans. Rodney Livingstone. 1971. Cambridge: MIT P, 1999.

Luke, Carmen, and Jennifer Gore, eds. *Feminisms and Critical Pedagogy.* New York: Routledge, 1992.

Lunsford, Andrea A. "Rhetoric and Composition." *Introduction to Scholarship in Modern Languages and Literatures.* Ed. Joseph Gibaldi. 2nd ed. New York: MLA, 1992. 77–102.

Massumi, Brian. *Parables for the Virtual.* Durham: Duke UP, 2002.

McGee, Sharon James, and Carolyn Handa. *Discord and Direction: The Postmodern Writing Program Administrator.* Logan: Utah State UP, 2005.

Micciche, Laura R. *Doing Emotion: Rhetoric, Writing, Teaching.* Portsmouth, NH: Boynton/Cook, 2007.

———. "More than a Feeling: Disappointment and WPA Work." *College English* 64 (2002): 432–58.

Miller, Richard E. *As If Learning Mattered: Reforming Higher Education.* Ithaca, NY: Cornell UP, 1998.

———. "Critique's the Easy Part: Choice and the Scale of Relative Oppression." George 3–13.

Miller, Scott L., Brenda Jo Brueggeman, Dennis Blue, and Deneen M. Shepherd. "Present Perfect and Future Imperfect: Results of a National Survey of Graduate Students in Rhetoric and Composition Programs." *CCC* 48.3 (1997): 392–409.

Miller, Susan. *Textual Carnivals: The Politics of Composition.* Carbondale: Southern Illinois UP, 1991.

Mouffe, Chantal. "Hegemony and New Political Subjects: Toward a New Concept of Democracy." Trans. Stanley Gray. *Marxism and the Interpretation of Culture.* Ed. Cary Nelson and Lawrence Grossberg. Urbana: U of Illinois P, 1988. 89–101.

———. "Rethinking Political Community: Chantal Mouffe's Liberal Socialism." Interview by Lynn Worsham and Gary A. Olson. *JAC: A Journal of Composition Theory* 19 (1999): 163–99.

Neuner, John J. W., and Benjamin R. Haynes. *Office Management and Practices.* Cincinnati: South-western, 1941.

Newfield, Christopher. *Ivy and Industry: Business and the Making of the American University, 1880–1980.* Durham, NC: Duke UP, 2004.

North, Stephen M. *The Making of Knowledge in Composition: Portrait of an Emerging Field.* Portsmouth, NH: Boynton/Cook, 1987.

Nystrand, Martin, et al. "Where Did Composition Studies Come From? An Intellectual History." *Written Communication* 10 (1993): 267–333.

"Objectives and Organization of the Composition Course." *CCC* 1.2 (May 1950): 9–14.

Ohmann, Richard. *English in America: A Radical View of the Profession.* 1976. Hanover, NH: UP of New England, 1996.

Olson, Gary A. "Critical Pedagogy and Composition Scholarship." *CCC* 48 (1997): 297–303.

O'Neill, Peggy, Angela Crow, and Larry W. Burton, eds. *A Field of Dreams: Independent Writing Programs and the Future of Composition Studies.* Logan: Utah State UP, 2002.

Paine, Charles. *The Resistant Writer: Rhetoric as Immunity, 1850 to the Present.* Albany: State U of New York P, 1999.

Parks, Stephen. *Class Politics: The Movement for the Students' Right to Their Own Language.* Urbana, IL: NCTE, 1999.

Pickett, Nell Ann. "The Two-Year College as Democracy in Action." *CCC* 49 (1998): 90–98.

Porter, Jim. "Re: Neo-Marxist Lightweight Takes on Rhet/Comp Swearingen." H-Rhetor Discussion Logs. H-Net Discussion Networks, 4 Feb. 2004. Web. 23 Feb. 2011.

Pringle, Rosemary. *Secretaries Talk: Sexuality, Power and Work.* New York: Verso, 1989.

"The Professional Status of the Composition Teacher." *CCC* 3.2 (Oct. 1952): 10–12.

Rabinbach, Anson. *The Human Motor: Energy, Fatigue, and the Origins of Modernity.* Berkeley: U of California P, 1990.

Ratcliffe, Krista, and Rebecca Rickly. *Performing Feminism and Administration in Rhetoric and Composition.* Cresskill, NJ: Hampton, 2010.

"The Report of Workshop No. 3A." *CCC* 1.2 (May 1950): 11–14.

Rhoades, Gary. *Managed Professionals: Unionized Faculty and Restructuring Academic Labor.* Albany: State U of New York P, 1998.

Rhodes, Keith. "Rhetoric, Pragmatism, Quality Management: Managing Better Writing." *Market Matters: Applied Rhetoric Studies and Free Market Composition.* Ed. Locke Carter. Cresskill, NJ: Hampton, 2005. 95–108.

Rice, Jeff. "Conservative Writing Program Administrators." Strickland and Gunner 1–13.

———. *The Rhetoric of Cool: Composition Studies and New Media.* Carbondale: Southern Illinois UP, 2007.

Rice, Thurman B. *Racial Hygiene: A Practical Discussion of Eugenics and Race Culture.* New York: Macmillan, 1929.

Ritter, Kelly. *Before Shaughnessy: Basic Writing at Harvard and Yale, 1920-1960.* Carbondale: Southern Illinois UP, 2009.

Rose, Shirley K. "Representing the Intellectual Work of Writing Program Administration: Professional Narratives of George Wykoff at Purdue, 1933–1967." L'Eplattenier and Mastrangelo 221–38.

Rose, Shirley K., and Irwin Weiser. *The Writing Program Administrator as Researcher: Inquiry in Action and Reflection.* Portsmouth, NH: Heinemann-Boynton/Cook, 1999.

————. *The Writing Program Administrator as Theorist: Making Knowledge Work*. Portsmouth, NH: Heinemann-Boynton/Cook, 2002.

Royster, Jacqueline Jones. *Traces of a Stream: Literacy and Social Change among African American Women*. Pittsburgh: U of Pittsburgh P, 2000.

————. "When the First Voice You Hear Is Not Your Own." *CCC* 47 (1996): 29–40.

Rutland, J. R. "Tendencies in the Administration of Freshman English." *English Journal* 12 (1923): 1–10.

Saxton, Alexander. *The Rise and Fall of the White Republic: Class Politics and Mass Culture in Nineteenth-Century America*. London: Verso, 1991.

Schell, Eileen E. "The Cost of Caring: 'Femininism' and Contingent Women Workers in Composition Studies." *Feminism and Composition Studies: In Other Words*. Ed. Susan C. Jarratt and Lynn Worsham. New York: MLA, 1998. 74–93.

————. *Gypsy Academics and Mother-Teachers: Gender, Contingent Labor, and Writing Instruction*. Portsmouth, NH: Heinemann-Boynton/ Cook, 1998.

Schuster, Charles I. "The Politics of Promotion." Bullock and Trimbur 85–95.

Scott, Fred N., ed. *The Philosophy of Style, Together with an Essay on Style by T. H. Wright*. By Herbert Spencer. Boston: Allyn and Bacon, 1892.

Scott, Tony. *Dangerous Writing: Understanding the Political Economy of Composition*. Logan: Utah State UP, 2009.

Selfe, Cynthia L. "Technology and Literacy: A Story about the Perils of Not Paying Attention." *CCC* 50 (1999): 411–36.

Shaughnessy, Mina. *Errors and Expectations: A Guide for the Teacher of Basic Writing*. New York: Oxford UP, 1977.

Shor, Ira. *Critical Teaching and Everyday Life*. 1980. Chicago: U of Chicago P, 1987.

Sirc, Geoffrey. *English Composition as a Happening*. Logan: Utah State UP, 2002.

Slaughter, Sheila, and Larry L. Leslie. *Academic Capitalism: Politics, Policies, and the Entrepreneurial University*. Baltimore: Johns Hopkins UP, 1999.

Spencer, Ellen Lane. *The Efficient Secretary*. New York: Frederick A. Stokes, 1916.

Stewart, Donald C., and Patricia L. Stewart. *The Life and Legacy of Fred Newton Scott*. Pittsburgh: U of Pittsburgh P, 1997.

Strickland, Donna. "Errors and Interpretations: Toward an Archaeology of Basic Writing." *Composition Studies* 26 (1998): 21–35.

————. "How to Compose a Capitalist: The Predicament of Required Writing in a Free Market Curriculum." *Composition Forum* 9 (1998): 25–38.

———. "Making the Managerial Conscious in Composition Studies." *American Academic* 1 (2004): 125–37.

Strickland, Donna, and Jeanne Gunner, eds. *The Writing Program Interrupted: Making Space for Critical Discourse.* Portsmouth, NH: Boynton/Cook-Heinemann, 2009.

Strom, Sharon Hartman. *Beyond the Typewriter: Gender, Class, and the Origins of Modern American Office Work, 1900–1930.* Urbana: U of Illinois P, 1992.

Stygall, Gail. "Women and Language in the Collaborative Writing Classroom." Jarratt and Worsham 252–75.

Swearingen, C. Jan. "Re: Neo-Marxist Lightweight Takes on Rhet/Comp Swearingen." H-Rhetor Discussion Logs. H-Net Discussion Networks, 9 Feb. 2004. Web. 16 Feb. 2011.

Taylor, Warner. *A National Survey of Conditions in Freshman English.* 1929. Brereton, *Origins* 545–62.

Thompson, Stith. "A National Survey of Freshman English." *English Journal* 19 (1930): 553–57.

Townsend, Kim. *Manhood at Harvard: William James and Others.* New York: Norton, 1996.

Trend, David. Introduction. *Radical Democracy: Identity, Citizenship, and the State.* New York: Routledge, 1996. 1–4.

Trimbur, John. "Literacy and the Discourse of Crisis." Bullock and Trimbur 277–95.

Varnum, Robin. "The History of Composition: Reclaiming Our Lost Generations." *Journal of Advanced Composition* 12 (1992): 39–55.

Webb, Janette. "Quality Management and the Management of Quality." Wilkinson and Willmott 105–26.

Weiner, Harvey. "President's Message." *WPA: Writing Program Administration* 4.3 (1981): 7.

White, Hayden. *Metahistory: The Historical Imagination in Nineteenth-Century Europe.* Baltimore: Johns Hopkins UP, 1975.

Whitney, Norman J. "Ability Grouping at Syracuse." *English Journal* 13 (1924): 482–89.

Wilkinson, Adrian, and Hugh Willmott, eds. *Making Quality Critical: New Perspectives on Organizational Change.* London: Routledge, 1995.

Williams, Blanche Colton. "Who Should Teach English?" *College English* 1 (1939): 406–14.

Williams, Raymond. *Keywords: A Vocabulary of Culture and Society.* Revised ed. New York: Oxford UP, 1985.

Woods, William F. "Industrial Management and Teaching Evaluation Programs." *WPA: Writing Program Administration* 3.2 (1979): 9–16.

Worsham, Lynn. "Going Postal: Pedagogic Violence and the Schooling of Emotion." *JAC: A Journal of Composition Theory* 18 (1998): 213–45.

Wykoff, George S. "Teaching Composition as a Career." *College English* 1 (1940): 426–37.

———. "Toward Achieving the Objectives of Freshman Composition." *College English* 10.6 (Mar. 1949): 319–23.

Yates, JoAnne. *Control through Communication: The Rise of System in American Management.* Baltimore: Johns Hopkins UP, 1989.

Zelnick, Stephen C. "A Report on the Workshop of the Administration of Writing Programs, Summer 1982." *WPA: Writing Program Administration* 6.3 (1983): 11–14.

Žižek, Slavoj. *The Sublime Object of Ideology.* New York: Verso, 1989.

# INDEX

**Donna Strickland** is an assistant professor of English and an associate director of composition at the University of Missouri–Columbia. With Jeanne Gunner, she has coedited *The Writing Program Interrupted: Making Space for Critical Discourse.*

## CCCC STUDIES IN WRITING & RHETORIC
*Edited by Joseph Harris, Duke University*

The aim of the CCCC Studies in Writing & Rhetoric (SWR) series is to influence how writing gets taught at the college level. The methods of studies vary from the critical to historical to linguistic to ethnographic, and their authors draw on work in various fields that inform composition—including rhetoric, communication, education, discourse analysis, psychology, cultural studies, and literature. Their focuses are similarly diverse—ranging from individual writers and teachers to classrooms and communities and curricula, to analyses of the social, political, and material contexts of writing and its teaching. Still, all SWR volumes try in some way to inform the practice of writing students, teachers, or administrators. Their approach is synthetic, their style concise and pointed. Complete manuscripts run from 40,000 to 50,000 words, or about 150–200 pages. Authors should imagine their work in the hands of writing teachers, as well as on library shelves.

SWR was one of the first scholarly book series to focus on the teaching of writing. It was established in 1980 by the Conference on College Composition and Communication (CCCC) to promote research in the emerging field of writing studies. Since its inception, the series has been copublished by Southern Illinois University Press. As the field has grown, the research sponsored by SWR has continued to articulate the commitment of CCCC to supporting the work of writing teachers as reflective practitioners and intellectuals. For a list of previous SWR books, see the SWR link on the SIU Press website at www.siupress.com.

We are eager to identify influential work in writing and rhetoric as it emerges. We thus ask authors to send us project proposals that clearly situate their work in the field and show how they aim to redirect our ongoing conversations about writing and its teaching. Proposals should include an overview of the project, a brief annotated table of contents, and a sample chapter. They should not exceed 10,000 words.

To submit a proposal or to contact the series editor, please go to http://uwp.aas.duke.edu/cccc/swr/.

## OTHER BOOKS IN THE CCCC STUDIES IN WRITING & RHETORIC SERIES

*African American Literacies Unleashed: Vernacular English and the Composition Classroom*
Arnetha F. Ball and Ted Lardner

*Digital Griots: African American Rhetoric in a Multimedia Age*
Adam J. Banks

*Rhetoric and Reality: Writing Instruction in American Colleges, 1900–1985*
James A. Berlin

*Writing Instruction in Nineteenth-Century American Colleges*
James A. Berlin

*Something Old, Something New: College Writing Teachers and Classroom Change*
Wendy Bishop

*The Variables of Composition: Process and Product in a Business Setting*
Glenn J. Broadhead and Richard C. Freed

*Audience Expectations and Teacher Demands*
Robert Brooke and John Hendricks

*Archives of Instruction: Nineteenth-Century Rhetorics, Readers, and Composition Books in the United States*
Jean Ferguson Carr, Stephen L. Carr, and Lucille M. Schultz

*Rehearsing New Roles: How College Students Develop as Writers*
Lee Ann Carroll

*Dialogue, Dialectic, and Conversation: A Social Perspective on the Function of Writing*
Gregory Clark

*Toward a Grammar of Passages*
Richard M. Coe

*A Communion of Friendship: Literacy, Spiritual Practice, and Women in Recovery*
Beth Daniell

*Rural Literacies*
Kim Donehower, Charlotte Hogg, and Eileen E. Schell

*Embodied Literacies: Imageword and a Poetics of Teaching*
Kristie S. Fleckenstein

*Writing with Authority: Students' Roles as Writers in Cross-National Perspective*
David Foster

*Writing Groups: History, Theory, and Implications*
Anne Ruggles Gere

*Sexuality and the Politics of Ethos in the Writing Classroom*
Zan Meyer Gonçalves

*Teaching/Writing in Thirdspaces: The Studio Approach*
Rhonda C. Grego and Nancy S. Thompson

*Computers & Composing: How the New Technologies Are Changing Writing*
Jeanne W. Halpern and Sarah Liggett

*Teaching Writing as a Second Language*
Alice S. Horning

*Revisionary Rhetoric, Feminist Pedagogy, and Multigenre Texts*
Julie Jung